SKI TOURS
in the
SIERRA NEVADA

Volume 1
Lake Tahoe

Marcus Libkind

Bittersweet Publishing Company
Livermore, California

Front cover photograph by David Giese: Descending to Sayles Canyon.

Rear cover photograph by Lee Griffith.

All other photographs by author unless noted otherwise.

Acknowledgment: Over the years many people have been the source of invaluable information. They include United States Forest Service personnel, California Department of Parks and Recreation personnel, the owners and operators of Nordic centers and mountain shops, friends, and acquaintances.

Library of Congress Catalog Card Number: 94-78552
International Standard Book Number: 0-931255-08-2

Published by Bittersweet Publishing Company
P.O. Box 1211, Livermore, California 94551

Printed in the United States of America on recycled paper

To

Sophie

Joyous are the days spent showing you the wilderness.
Father teaching daughter; daughter opening father's eyes.

Contents

INTRODUCTION 8

THE BACKCOUNTRY EXPERIENCE 9

AUTHOR'S NOTE 11

HOW TO USE THIS BOOK 12

DONNER-TRUCKEE

   Area Map 19

    1 Nancy Lake 20
    2 Snow Mountain 24
    3 Fisher Lake Overlook 27
    4 High Loch Leven Lake 30
    5 High Loch Leven Lake-Rainbow Loop 32
    6 Lower Lola Montez Lake 34
    7 Cascade Lakes 37
    8 Crows Nest 39
    9 The Cedars 41
  10 Mount Judah and Donner Peak 44
  11 Mount Judah Loop 46
  12 Sugar Bowl to Squaw Valley 50
  13 Lakes Crossing 52
  14 Donner Pass Road to Interstate 80 via Boreal Ridge 54
  15 Andesite Peak 55
  16 Andesite Ridge Loop 56
  17 Castle Valley Loop 58
  18 Round Valley and Peter Grubb Hut 60
  19 Castle Peak 62
  20 Donner Pass to Highway 89 via Mt. Lola 63
  21 Summit Lake 70
  22 Frog Lake Cliff 73
  23 Donner Memorial State Park 74
  24 Coldstream Valley 76
  25 Schallenberger Loop 78
  26 Schallenberger Ridge 80
  27 Highway 89 North of Truckee 82
  28 Sagehen Hills 84
  29 Stampede Reservoir Overlook 87
  30 Kyburz Flat and Wheelers Sheep Camp Loop 88
  31 Kyburz Flat Big Loop 90
  32 Sardine Peak 93

NORTH TAHOE

Area Map 97

33 Cabin Creek Loop 98
34 Pole Creek Loop 102
35 Saddle Trail Loop 104
36 Silver Peak 106
37 Truckee River 108
38 Paige Meadows 111
39 Scott Peak 112
40 Stanford Rock 114
41 Blackwood Canyon 117
42 Barker Pass 119
43 Miller Meadows 120
44 Richardson Lake 124
45 McKinney Creek and General Creek Loop 126
46 Sugar Pine Point State Park 128
47 General Creek 130
48 Meeks Creek 131
49 Painted Rock Loop 132
50 Tahoe City to Truckee 138
51 Brockway Summit to Agate Bay 140
52 Brockway Summit to Tahoe City 142
53 Brockway Summit to Northstar 146
54 Martis Peak 148
55 Martis Peak and Mt. Baldy Traverse 152
56 Northstar to Lake Tahoe via Mt. Pluto 155
57 Tahoe Meadows 159
58 Mt. Rose Highway to Brockway Summit 160
59 Third Creek Loop 165
60 Tahoe Meadows to Incline 166

SOUTH TAHOE

Area Map 169

61 Angora Lookout and Angora Lakes 170
62 Fallen Leaf Lake from Tahoe Mountain Road 172
63 Fallen Leaf Lake from Highway 89 173
64 Mt. Tallac Direct 174
65 Mt. Tallac's North Ridge 175
66 Mt. Tallac to Fallen Leaf Lake 178
67 Fountain Place 180
68 Freel Peak 181
69 Meyers to Hope Valley 184
70 High Meadows 186

SOUTH TAHOE (continued)

71 Star Lake 189
72 Kingsbury Grade to Spooner Junction 190
73 Government Meadow 194
74 Big Meadow 195
75 Scotts Lake 198
76 Round Lake and Dardanelles Lake 200
77 Grass Lake 202
78 Grass Lake to Meyers 203
79 Thompson Peak 205
80 Grass Lake to Hope Valley via Thompson Peak 208
81 Luther Pass to Hope Valley 209

ECHO SUMMIT

Area Map 211

82 Robbs Peak 212
83 Berts Lake and Peak 6836 215
84 Chipmunk Bluff 217
85 South Shore of Loon Lake 218
86 North Shore of Loon Lake 220
87 Strawberry Canyon Road 221
88 Strawberry Ridge Loop 222
89 Station Creek Trail 225
90 Cody Creek Loop 228
91 Cody Meadow Loop 230
92 Packsaddle Pass 232
93 Echo Summit 233
94 Becker Peak 234
95 Echo Lakes 236
96 Echo Peak 237
97 Desolation Valley 238
98 Echo Summit to Fallen Leaf Lake 242
99 Lake Audrian 244
100 Huckleberry Ridge 246
101 Sayles Canyon 250
102 Benwood Meadow 252

NORDIC SKI CENTERS

NORDIC SKI CENTERS 254

UPDATES 256

Introduction

The guidebook series, *Ski Tours in the Sierra Nevada*, forms a comprehensive collection of ski tours which I have encountered during more than two decades of exploring the Sierra. They range geographically from the Lake Tahoe region in the north to Sequoia National Park in the south. The Lake Tahoe, Carson Pass, Bear Valley, Pinecrest, Yosemite, Huntington and Shaver Lakes, Kings Canyon and Sequoia, and eastern Sierra areas are all covered in depth.

Whether you are a novice or an old timer, this series of guidebooks will introduce you to new and interesting areas which offer excellent ski touring. The information in these volumes will be useful for planning tours of an appropriate difficulty so you can enjoy more pleasurable and safer touring.

The 102 tours in this volume cover the Lake Tahoe region and are divided as follows:

> DONNER-TRUCKEE — Tours originating from or near Interstate 80. Includes tours from or near Highway 89 north of Interstate 80, but does not include Highway 89 south of Interstate 80 nor does it include Highway 267.

> NORTH TAHOE — Tours originating from or near Highway 89 south of Interstate 80 and north of Meeks Creek, Highway 28 west of Incline Village, and Highways 267 and 431.

> SOUTH TAHOE — Tours originating from or near Highway 89 south of Meeks Creek and north of Luther Pass, Highway 50 north of Meyers, and Highway 28 south of Incline Village.

> ECHO SUMMIT — Tours originating from or near Highway 50 west of Meyers.

Although you may have the tendency to skip to and begin reading the tour descriptions, I hope you will take a few minutes to read the next three sections: The Backcountry Experience gives you a glimpse of my philosophy in backcountry skiing. Author's Note and How To Use This Book are important to your safety and understanding of how to use this guidebook.

I sincerely hope that the tours in these guidebooks will inspire you to explore new areas. I have thoroughly enjoyed the time spent in researching these books and I will be rewarded each time I meet another ski tourer who has found this information useful. Please let me know your comments and suggestions.

Marcus Libkind
P.O. Box 1211
Livermore, California 94551

The Backcountry Experience

What can you expect off the beaten path of track skiing? Sheltered bowls that beckon you to carve the first tracks in the hillside, windswept summits where you can lunch among spectacular vistas, a creek you can glide alongside while savoring winter's beauty — the surprises are innumerable.

Although traveling in the backcountry is a slower process than following groomed trails, you gain the solitude and freedom of choosing your own route among the magnificent and unspoiled Sierra. If you feel uncertain about your map and compass skills, or decide that route-finding is too worrisome a task, you can still enjoy backcountry skiing by relying on friends to be your guide or by participating in organized group tours.

However, if you feel confident enough to strike out on your own, this guidebook contains valuable information for planning a backcountry tour.

Not all backcountry ski routes are difficult to follow. Choose a tour on snow-covered roads or marked but ungroomed trails if you have no experience navigating with a map and compass. Bring along the appropriate topographic map and a compass, and develop your ability to interpret the contour lines and to locate landmarks and your position from the terrain. You can tackle more difficult and challenging routes after you have mastered these basic route-finding skills.

If you are planning your very first experience in the backcountry, consider these suggestions to ensure your safe trip: Pick a relatively short tour and allow extra time to complete it. Remember, five miles of backcountry skiing will take much longer than it would on a groomed track. Choose a tour from which you can easily return. If the terrain is more difficult than you had anticipated, if the weather takes a turn for the worse, or if the route-finding becomes too difficult, you should turn back immediately. Unfortunately, you cannot depend on following your own tracks out since they can be covered by windblown snow or a new snowfall. You should also inquire locally about current avalanche conditions, or better yet, learn to recognize them. Finally, never ski alone and always let a responsible person know where you are going and when you plan to return.

In the backcountry, expect to encounter a variety of snow conditions, from ice to slush, for which the Sierra is notorious. Also, do not be surprised if your track skiing techniques are somewhat inadequate for backcountry terrain. To enjoy backcountry skiing, you may need to refine your old techniques and learn new ones, such as climbing in deep, untracked powder, traversing steep slopes and turning without the aid of a groomed track.

You do not need special equipment, such as metal-edged skis or heavy boots, to enjoy backcountry skiing. With lighter equipment, you can ski with greater ease and comfort. If you are considering renting or purchasing equipment for backcountry skiing, look for equipment that gives you greater control for maneuvering on ungroomed slopes. Inquire about wider skis that have a soft camber and pronounced side-cut; sturdy, torsionally rigid, ankle-high boots are desirable for more support and control; and although the author still prefers 75-millimeter Nordic norm bindings, there are other boot-binding systems that will work very satisfactorily.

Regardless of whether your equipment is old, new or rented, always make sure that every piece is in good repair. Check that your bindings are attached firmly to your skis, that neither your skis nor poles are cracked, and that the soles of your boots are not falling apart.

Since you must be self-sufficient when traveling in the backcountry, make sure that you or your group is carrying all the basic items such as sunscreen, sunglasses, first aid kit, matches and fire starter or candle, flashlight, combination pocketknife, map and compass, food, extra clothing, plenty of water and toilet paper. A small waterproof tarp is very useful in emergencies and adds comfort to your lunch stop. For additional comfort, you can splurge and carry a small piece of closed-cell foam to sit on.

The conditions on every tour, no matter where it is located, will be different from day to day; somedays great, somedays good, and somedays poor. But on any day there are good, or at least better, tours. Knowing which one to choose is a learned skill.

Here are things you should consider when picking a tour. Skiing may be better at a low elevation during or soon after a heavy snowfall. An extremely cold storm is another good opportunity to do a low elevation tour. New snow, at low elevations, quickly turns to mush after the storm passes. However, that snow consolidates quickly. South-facing slopes, at any elevation, turn to heavy mush soon after a storm. North-facing slopes, at any elevation, retain powder conditions much longer. It goes without saying that there are other considerations too.

Plan as many tours as you can for spring, corn-snow conditions. Corn-snow is created after well-consolidated snow melts and re-freezes many times. I consider this the best skiing the Sierra has to offer. The days are longer than in winter, travel is easier and faster, and turning is a dream. This is the time to practice linking turns or to enjoy those big descents. Some people call it "ego snow."

Flexibility is a key factor in optimizing the quality of your tours. Be prepared to change your plans in the event of a new snowfall or a drastic change in temperatures.

Finally, ski as often as you can. Not only will your technique improve, but you will be more likely to experience those elusive "perfect" days.

Careful and conscientious planning will maximize your enjoyment and minimize the dangers in the wilderness. The self-confidence you develop from traveling in the wilderness, the sense of excitement and adventure that accompanies each backcountry tour, and the sheer unspoiled winter beauty of the Sierra are the rewards.

Author's Note

There are certain inherent dangers associated with wilderness travel in winter. No guidebook can diminish the hazards nor be a guarantee of safety. If you choose to experience the mountains in winter, you voluntarily do so knowing there are hazards.

Although the tour descriptions make reference to specific, obvious dangers, you should not assume that they are the only ones. Even the safest tour can become dangerous should you encounter poor weather, poor snow, or avalanche conditions.

Some tours may take you through private property which is not marked. If you encounter marked private property, I hope that you will respect the property rights of others so that the good reputation of ski tourers will be preserved. Similarly, some tours pass through downhill ski resorts. For safety and to promote continued goodwill, it is important to stay off the groomed slopes when ascending.

Although great care has gone into researching the tours in this guidebook, you may find inconsistencies due to factors such as new construction of roads and housing, policies toward plowing roads, changes in parking restrictions, and changes in trail markers. Also, extreme variations in snowfall can make a remarkable difference in how things appear. Be prepared to cope with these discrepancies should they arise.

In the final analysis, you must be responsible for executing your own safe trip.

A book comforts author while he waits for helicopter   by Keith Kishiyama

How To Use This Book

The short time it takes you to read this section will increase the usefulness of this guidebook. Each tour description in this guidebook contains a summary, an introduction, and a mileage log. The summary box gives you at a glance the significant characteristics of the tour. The introduction describes the aesthetic features of the tour, special considerations, alternate routes, and general information which will be helpful in planning a tour. The mileage log describes the route in an easy-to-follow format.

Summary Box

Difficulty: The difficulty ratings are based on four criteria: length, elevation change, steepness, and navigation. A five level scale for rating the overall difficulty of the tours is used. The skills associated with each level are:

1 – Beginner
  - Little or no previous ski touring experience
  - Ability to follow simple directions without map or compass

2 – Advanced beginner
  - Proficiency in the basic techniques: diagonal stride, side-step, kick turn, step turn, snowplow, and snowplow turn
  - Ability to control speed on gradual downhills
  - Ability to negotiate short, moderately steep sections of terrain
  - Ability to follow simple directions in conjunction with a map

3 – Intermediate
  - Excellent proficiency in all the basic techniques plus the traverse and herringbone on moderately steep terrain
  - Ability to negotiate long, moderately steep, and short, steep sections of terrain
  - Good stamina
  - Ability to navigate using a topographic map
  - Ability to use a compass to determine general orientation

4 – Advanced intermediate
  - Excellent proficiency in all ski touring techniques
  - Ability to negotiate long, steep sections of terrain including densely wooded areas
  - Strong skier
  - Ability to navigate using a topographic map and compass

5 – Expert
  - Excellent all around skier and mountain person
  - Ability to negotiate very steep terrain
  - Exceptional endurance
  - Ability to navigate using a topographic map and compass

Two tours may be assigned the same rating but vary greatly in the skills required. For example, both a tour on a road which is long and a tour which is short but requires navigation by map and compass may be rated 3. For this reason the difficulty ratings should only be used as a general guide for selecting a tour of appropriate difficulty. Check the summary box for information regarding length, elevation change, and navigation to determine whether your abilities match the demands of the tour. Also, refer to the introduction for special considerations.

The tours were rated assuming ideal snow conditions. Deep powder will make travel slower and more difficult. Ice will make all tours much more difficult. If faced with icy conditions in the morning, you might consider waiting until early afternoon to begin, when hopefully the snow will be thawed.

Length: The length is an estimate of the horizontal mileage as obtained from the topographic maps. Several of the tours are in meadows which are adjacent to plowed roads and in these cases the length is simply stated as "short." Whether the mileage is one-way or round trip is also noted.

Elevation: The first number is the elevation at the starting point of the tour in feet above sea level. The elevation is a major consideration when planning tours early or late in the season.

The elevation at the starting point is followed by a slash and the elevation change for the entire tour. The change is written as "+gain,–loss." "Nil" is used where the change is negligible.

Navigation: The navigational difficulty of each tour is based on untracked snow and good visibility. The key words and phrases are:

Adjacent to plowed road – Tour is located almost completely within sight of a plowed road.

Road – Tour follows snow-covered roads. Although roads are normally easy to follow, a small road or a road in open terrain may be difficult to locate or follow.

Marked trail – Tour follows marked trail; may require basic map-reading skills. Markers are normally brightly colored pieces of metal or plastic attached to trees, or strips of brightly colored ribbon attached to tree branches. Blazes which mark summer trails are not considered markers since they are often obscured by snow. Whenever you are on a marked trail, you must pay careful attention to locating each successive marker which may not be ideally placed. Even with a marked trail, you will probably need some knowledge of the route and basic map-reading skills to follow it.

Map – Tour requires the ability to read a topographic map since the tour follows well-defined terrain such as creeks, valleys, and ridges. Remember that poor visibility can make route-finding impossible without a compass and expert knowledge of its use.

Compass – Tour requires the use of a compass in conjunction with a topographic map. In some instances the compass is mainly for safety, but other routes require you to follow compass bearings.

Time: The following key words and phrases are used to give a general idea of the length of time required to complete a tour:

- Short
- Few hours
- Half day
- Most of a day
- Full day
- Very long day

Some of the factors which will affect your trip time include snow and weather conditions, your skiing ability and physical strength, characteristics of the tour, and your personal habits. I included time for reasonable rests and for route-finding in making my estimates.

Always keep in mind that the days are short in the mid-winter months. Very long tours are best done in early spring when the days are longer.

Climbing skin make steep climbs easy   by David Giese

Season: The season is the period in an average snowfall year during which the snow conditions for the tour are acceptable. Early and late in the season the conditions may be less than optimum. Exceptionally early or late snowfall as well as heavy snowfall extend the season. On the other hand, during drought years the season may be shortened.

USGS topo: The United States Geological Survey (USGS) no longer produces 15 minute series maps; only 7.5 minute series maps are available. Therefore, in all cases the appropriate 7.5 minute series maps are listed.

Parts of USGS maps are reproduced in this guidebook; the map reproduction number and its page location are at the beginning of each tour adjacent to the tour name. Be aware that the reproductions are reduced. The following is a legend for the reproduced topographic maps:

●   Start

■   Destination

5   Landmark number (corresponds to mileage log)

—— Ski route

—— Plowed road

USGS maps are available at most mountain shops, at the USGS office in Menlo Park, CA, and by mail from:

> United States Geological Survey
> Box 25286 Denver Federal Building
> Denver, Colorado 80225

Start and end: Described are detailed directions for locating the starting and ending points of the tour. The ending point is omitted if the tour route returns to where it began.

Keep in mind that it may not be legal to park at these points. It is your responsibility to determine whether it is legal to do so. Sometimes carrying a snow shovel will allow you to clear a place to park. At other times you may need to pay for parking or walk some distance.

The California "SnoPark" bill created a system of winter parking areas for winter sports users. It is noted whether the starting or ending points are SnoPark sites.

A permit is required to park at SnoPark sites. Both one-day and season permits are available at many mountain shops throughout California and other businesses in mountain communities. Permits are also available by mail from:

> SnoPark Program
> Department of Parks and Recreation
> P.O. Box 942896
> Sacramento, California 94296-0001
> (916) 653-8569

Mileage Log

The mileage log is designed to make it easy for you to follow the route description and keep track of your progress. Keep in mind that the description is not a substitute for knowledge, skill, and common sense. The following sample mileage log entry will help you understand how to read the log entries.

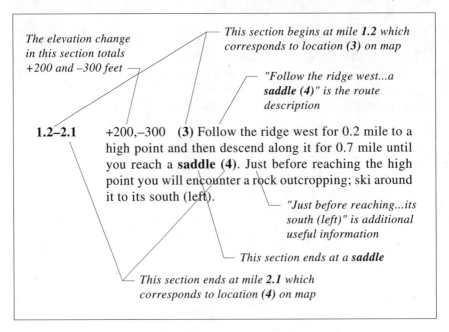

The elevation change in this section totals +200 and –300 feet

*This section begins at mile **1.2** which corresponds to location (**3**) on map*

*"Follow the ridge west...a **saddle (4)**" is the route description*

1.2–2.1   +200,–300   (**3**) Follow the ridge west for 0.2 mile to a high point and then descend along it for 0.7 mile until you reach a **saddle** (**4**). Just before reaching the high point you will encounter a rock outcropping; ski around it to its south (left).

"Just before reaching...its south (left)" is additional useful information

*This section ends at a **saddle***

*This section ends at mile **2.1** which corresponds to location (**4**) on map*

Volunteer trail marking

It's easy going when someone else breaks the trail

Donner-Truckee

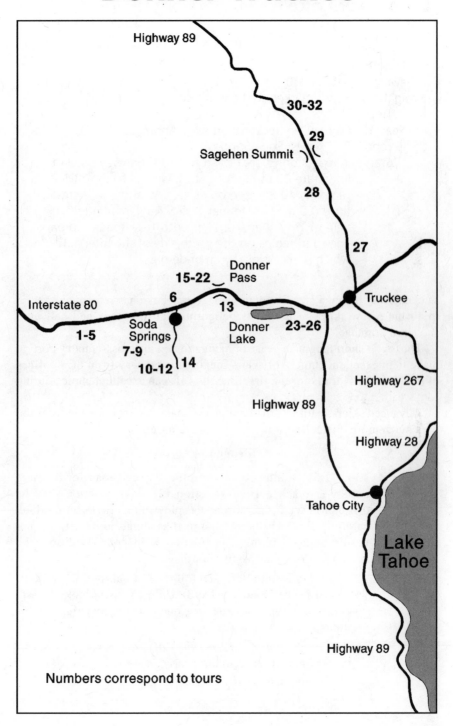

Highway 89

30-32

29

Sagehen Summit

28

27

Donner
Pass

15-22

6

Truckee

Interstate 80

13

Soda
Springs

Donner
Lake

23-26

1-5

7-9

10-12 14

Highway 267

Highway 89

Highway 28

Tahoe City

Lake
Tahoe

Highway 89

Numbers correspond to tours

1 Nancy Lake

Difficulty	3
Length	4 miles round trip
Elevation	6100/+700,–700
Navigation	Road, marked trail and map
Time	Half day
Season	Mid-December through early April
USGS topo	7.5' series, Soda Springs
Start	Intersection of Troy Road and Old Highway 40. Exit Interstate 80 at Kingvale, turn west (left) onto Old Highway 40 (located on north side of the interstate), drive 0.5 mile to Donner Trail School, continue 0.1 mile to Troy Road, turn left onto Troy Road, and park. The tour begins on the south side of the interstate which is accessible by an underpass.

Tucked away below a steep canyon wall, Nancy Lake has remained a secret to all but a few skiers. The tour is delightful, half on roads and half up a sheltered drainage.

The tour's short length and ease of navigation on the cross-country portion make it an excellent choice for skiers seeking to get away from the confines of roads and busy trails for the first time. It is also an excellent choice during foul weather.

Advanced skiers, with lots of stamina, can make Nancy Lake the first stop on a much more difficult tour to Snow Mountain (no. 2).

Mileage Log

0.0 – 0.1   +50 **(1)** Ski southwest on the snow-covered road for 0.1 mile until you reach a **road junction (2)**. This junction may be difficult to see if the railroad has plowed this first section; look carefully above the berm for a road heading south (left). Do not be discouraged if this first section is in poor condition; the snow-players do not venture farther.

0.1 – 0.7   +250 **(2)** Turn south (left) and follow the road for 0.6 mile until you reach the **railroad tracks (3)**. Unless you are looking hard, you will not notice that you pass one road on your right in this section.

> *Take off your skis and cross the railroad tracks. Be aware that in heavy snow years the berm on the south side of the tracks can be difficult to climb up.*

1

> *After crossing the tracks, locate the extension of the road on which you have been skiing. It is marked with a sign indicating the start of the High Loch Leven Lake Trail. That ski trail is described in the High Loch Leven Lake tour (no. 4).*

0.7 – 0.9 +50 **(3)** Ski on the road for 0.2 mile until you reach an obscure **road junction (4)**. However, just beyond the junction is one of Royal Gorge Cross Country Ski Resort's warming huts.

> *This tour follows the lesser road to the southwest which is marked with an arrow. You may also find a Royal Gorge sign indicating that the lesser road is part of the Rainbow Interconnect (trail). This road, even if groomed, is open to public travel.*

0.9 – 1.1 +100 **(4)** Turn west (right) onto the lesser road and climb southwest for 0.2 mile until you reach a **fork in the road (5)**. Although hard to see, the fork can be located by noting where the road you have been skiing on becomes significantly more steep. The fork is located there.

1.1 – 2.1 +200,–50 **(5)** Veer south (left) on the lesser road, descend into the creek drainage, and follow the drainage south for a total of 1.0 mile until you reach **Nancy Lake (6)**. The road will soon disappear, and you follow the creek and the drainage to the lake. Although you can ski on either side of the creek, crossing it where snow-covered, you should definitely move to the east (left) side of the drainage as you approach Nancy Lake. As you approach, there is a vertical wall on the west (right) side of the drainage.

A worthwhile, short extension of the tour to Nancy Lake entails continuing south for 0.2 mile until the terrain opens and becomes filled with a jumble of granite boulders and cliffs that make skiing difficult. Where the terrain opens, Snow Mountain is visible in the distance.

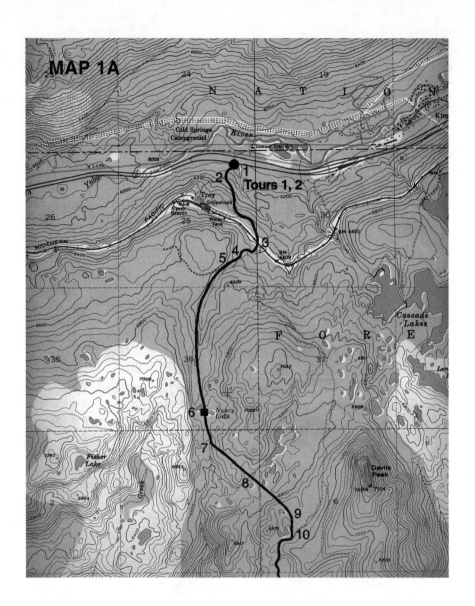

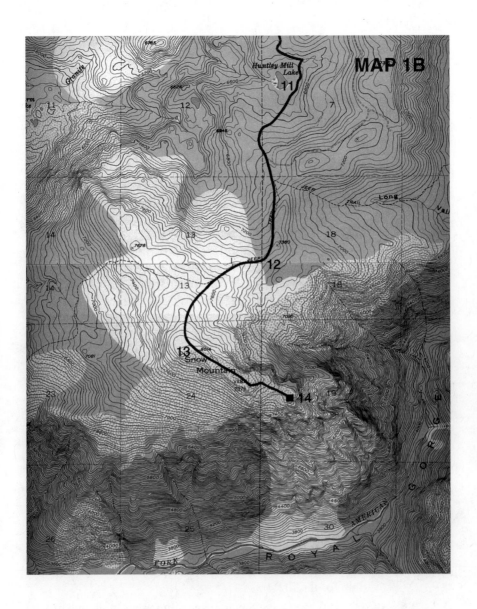

MAP 1B

2 Snow Mountain

PAGE 22-23

Difficulty	5
Length	14 miles round trip
Elevation	6100/+3000,–3000
Navigation	Road, marked trail, map and compass
Time	Very long day
Season	Mid-December through early April
USGS topo	7.5′ series, Soda Springs, Royal Gorge
Start	Intersection of Troy Road and Old Highway 40. Exit Interstate 80 at Kingvale, turn west (left) onto Old Highway 40 (located on north side of the interstate), drive 0.5 mile to Donner Trail School, continue 0.1 mile to Troy Road, turn left onto Troy Road, and park. The tour begins on the south side of the interstate which is accessible by an underpass.

Towering 4000 feet above the "Royal Gorge" of the North Fork of the American River, Snow Mountain commands a 360-degree panorama. Ski to the southeast end of its ridge and you look straight down to the river below.

The tour to Snow Mountain is very difficult, much more so than its 14 miles indicate. The need to continually navigate by map and compass, rocky terrain, and lots of elevation gain make it only suitable for strong, advanced skiers. But the rewards are great for those that make the journey.

Mileage Log

0.0 – 2.1 +650,–50 **(1)** Follow the Nancy Lake tour (no. 1) for 2.1 miles until you reach **Nancy Lake (6)**.

2.1 – 2.3 +0 **(6)** Ski south for 0.2 mile until the terrain opens and becomes filled with a jumble of **granite boulders and cliffs (7)** that make skiing difficult. Where the terrain opens, Snow Mountain is visible for the first time.

2.3 – 2.6 +100,–100 **(7)** Leave the drainage, climb onto a shoulder to the southeast, and then descend for a total of 0.3 mile until you reach a **creek (8)**. In low snow conditions, even this route is not much fun, but it is the best choice. You will get your first view of the Big Granite Creek drainage from the shoulder.

2.6 – 3.0 +200 **(8)** Cross the creek and climb southeast for 0.4 mile until you reach a **flat area (9)**. Nearby is Devils Peak and in the distance to the north are Castle and Basin peaks. This climb marks the beginning of more pleasant ski touring terrain.

24

2

3.0 – 3.1 +0 **(9)** Ski south for 0.1 mile until you reach a **lake (10)** near Peak 6979.

3.1 – 4.0 –200 **(10)** Continue south, hopefully picking up the road, and descend for a total of 0.9 mile until you reach **Huntley Mill Lake (11)**. At the lake you will probably lose the road.

4.0 – 5.3 +650 **(11)** Climb south, picking your route through trees and open areas, for 1.3 miles until you reach the **saddle (12)** southwest of Peak 7380.

5.3 – 6.3 +650 **(12)** Climb southwest and then south for a total of 1.0 mile until you reach the **northwest end of Snow Mountain (13)**.

6.3 – 7.0 –400 **(13)** Ski southeast along Snow Mountain's broad, flat ridge for 0.4 mile and then descend for 0.3 mile until you reach the **cliff (14)** above the North Fork of the American River. There is a patch of trees at the end of the ridge where the cliff is located.

Descending from Snow Mountain

Scenery along High Loch Leven Lake Trail

MAP 2
PAGE 29

Fisher Lake Overlook **3**

Difficulty	3
Length	6 miles round trip
Elevation	6100/+1200,–1200
Navigation	Road, marked trail and map
Time	Most of a day
Season	Mid-December through early April
USGS topo	7.5′ series, Soda Springs
Start	Intersection of Troy Road and Old Highway 40. Exit Interstate 80 at Kingvale, turn west (left) onto Old Highway 40 (located on north side of the interstate), drive 0.5 mile to Donner Trail School, continue 0.1 mile to Troy Road, turn left onto Troy Road, and park. The tour begins on the south side of the interstate which is accessible by an underpass.

Fisher Lake and its overlook lie in the heart of the high plateau to the south of Interstate 80 near Kingvale. The marked High Loch Leven Lake Trail, established by volunteers in 1991, makes access to this superb touring area reasonable for intermediate skiers.

You will cover a mixture of terrain, both forested and open, on roads and cross-country, on the tour to Fisher Lake Overlook. The openness of the plateau, along with its lack of landmarks, makes this area a poor choice during inclement weather. Without good visibility, route-finding in the open areas would require expert dead-reckoning with a map and compass.

You will have two choices for returning from Fisher Lake Overlook. You can retrace your tracks or you can complete a loop around the perimeter of the plateau. More ambitious skiers can lengthen this tour by making High Loch Leven Lake (no. 4) their destination.

Mileage Log

0.0 – 0.1 +50 **(1)** Ski southwest on the snow-covered road for 0.1 mile until you reach a **road junction (2)**. This junction may be difficult to see if the railroad has plowed this first section; look carefully above the berm for a road heading south (left). Don't be discouraged if this first section is in poor condition; the snow-players do not venture farther.

0.1 – 0.7 +250 **(2)** Turn south (left) and follow the road for 0.6 mile until you reach the **railroad tracks (3)**. Unless you are looking hard, you will not notice that you pass one road on your right in this section.

3

Take off your skis and cross the railroad tracks. Be aware that in heavy snow years the berm on the south side of the tracks can be difficult to climb up.

After crossing the tracks, locate the extension of the road on which you have been skiing. It is marked with a sign indicating the start of the High Loch Leven Lake Trail.

0.7 – 0.9   +50 **(3)** Ski on the road for 0.2 mile until you reach an obscure **road junction (4)**. However, just beyond the junction is one of Royal Gorge Cross Country Ski Resort's warming huts.

This tour follows the lesser road to the southwest which is marked with an arrow. You may also find a Royal Gorge sign indicating that the lesser road is part of the Rainbow Interconnect (trail). This road, even if groomed, is open to public travel.

0.9 – 1.2   +150 **(4)** Turn west (right) onto the lesser road and climb southwest for 0.3 mile until you reach a **flat area (5)** where the marked backcountry ski trail and the Rainbow Interconnect split. The Rainbow Interconnect veers to the northwest (right) and the High Loch Leven Trail veers to the southwest (left).

1.2 – 1.9   +300 **(5)** Leave the road and follow the marked trail to the southwest for 0.7 mile until you enter a **clearing (6)**.

1.9 – 2.7   +200 **(6)** Ski southwest across the clearing, staying close to the trees to the north, and then veer south for a total of 0.8 mile until you intersect a **road (7)** to the west of a horseshoe-shaped pond. In this section you must exercise patience in locating each successive trail marker. They are few and far between.

The marked trail to High Loch Leven Lake follows the road to the west (right). The tour to Fisher Lake Overlook leaves the marked trail and road, and continues south.

2.7 – 2.9   +100 **(7)** Ski south on level terrain for 0.1 mile and then climb south for 0.1 mile until you reach **Fisher Lake Overlook (8)**.

You can return to the starting point by retracing your tracks or you can make a loop as described below.

2.9 – 3.6   +100,–300 **(8)** Ski northeast, skirting the perimeter of the plateau, for 0.7 mile until you reach **Peak 7000 (9)**. In this section you must loop around a gully.

3.6 – 3.8   –100 **(9)** Descend north for 0.2 mile until you intersect the **marked trail (6)** near where it entered the clearing.

3.8 – 5.7   –800 **(6)** Retrace your route for 1.9 miles back to the **starting point (1)**.

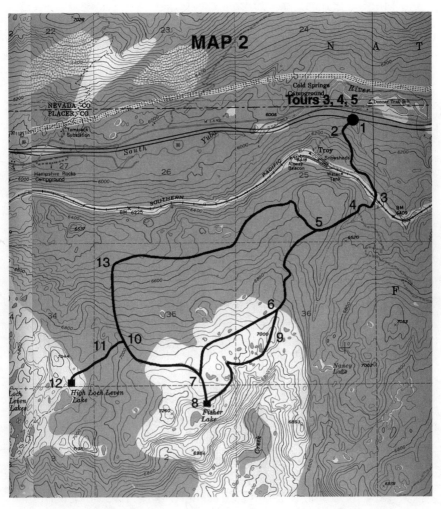

MAP 2
PAGE 29

4 High Loch Leven Lake

Difficulty	3
Length	8 miles round trip
Elevation	6100/+1250,−1250
Navigation	Road, marked trail and map
Time	Most of a day
Season	Mid-December through early April
USGS topo	7.5' series, Soda Springs
Start	Intersection of Troy Road and Old Highway 40. Exit Interstate 80 at Kingvale, turn west (left) onto Old Highway 40 (located on north side of the interstate), drive 0.5 mile to Donner Trail School, continue 0.1 mile to Troy Road, turn left onto Troy Road, and park. The tour begins on the south side of the interstate which is accessible by an underpass.

Established in 1991 by volunteers, the High Loch Leven Lake Trail climbs from Interstate 80 near Kingvale and then crosses a high plateau before reaching its terminus above High Loch Leven Lake. The climbing, considerable at first, is an investment that pays off when you ski across the rolling, sometimes open, sometimes forested terrain of the plateau.

Like the nearby, shorter Fisher Lake Overlook tour (no. 3), the openness along this tour make it a poor choice in foul weather. But pick a clear, crisp day and you will enjoy not only the touring, but also the grand views to the south.

The tour to High Loch Leven Lake can be combined with the Fisher Lake Overlook tour. Also, the High Loch Leven Lake-Rainbow Loop tour (no. 5) combines this tour to the lake with a return via Royal Gorge Cross Country Ski Resort's Rainbow Interconnect (trail).

Mileage Log

0.0 – 2.7   +1000 **(1)** Follow the Fisher Lake Overlook Loop tour (no. 3) for 2.7 miles until you reach the **road (7)** west of a horseshoe-shaped pond.

2.7 – 3.3   −100 **(7)** Turn west (right) onto the road, and ski west for 0.4 mile and then north for 0.2 mile until you reach a **road junction (10)**.The road that continues north (straight) is part of the High Loch Leven Lake-Rainbow Loop tour. This tour follows the road that turns west (left).

3.3 – 3.4   −50 **(10)** Turn west (left) and ski 0.1 mile until you reach a **flat, open area (11)** where the road turns south (left).

4

Locate the marker that indicates where the marked trail leaves the road to the southwest.

3.4 – 3.8 +50,–50 **(11)** Leave the road and ski southwest, following the markers, for 0.4 mile until you reach the end of the marked trail above **High Loch Leven Lake (12)**. In this section the marked trail takes a circuitous route through a maze of trees and rocks.

Lunch stop

5 High Loch Leven Lake-Rainbow Loop

MAP 2
PAGE 29

Difficulty	3
Length	8 miles round trip
Elevation	6100/+1400,–1400
Navigation	Road, marked trail and map
Time	Most of a day
Season	Mid-December through early April
USGS topo	7.5' series, Soda Springs
Start	Intersection of Troy Road and Old Highway 40. Exit Interstate 80 at Kingvale, turn west (left) onto Old Highway 40 (located on north side of the interstate), drive 0.5 mile to Donner Trail School, continue 0.1 mile to Troy Road, turn left onto Troy Road, and park. The tour begins on the south side of the interstate which is accessible by an underpass.

This tour connects the High Loch Leven Lake tour (no. 4) with Royal Gorge Cross Country Ski Resort's Rainbow Interconnect (trail) to form a loop. The return is along a north-facing road, sheltered by forest, and offers a great contrast to the route in across the plateau. This is an excellent choice for your return when wind has caused icy conditions on the plateau.

Royal Gorge grooms the Rainbow Interconnect only when there is sufficient snow for their customers to ski down to Rainbow Lodge. That condition only exists during the middle of an average winter. If groomed, you are permitted to ski on the tracks in the section described in this tour. However, be aware that, for the resort patrons, the groomed trail is one-way in the opposite direction you will be skiing. Therefore, exercise caution and give way to oncoming skiers.

Mileage Log

0.0 – 3.8 +1050,–200 **(1)** Follow the High Loch Leven Lake tour (no. 4) for 3.8 miles until you reach the end of the marked trail above **High Loch Leven Lake (12)**.

3.8 – 4.3 +100,–50 **(12)** Retrace your tracks for 0.5 mile until you reach the last **road junction (10)**. Your old tracks will head south (right) on the road while this loop continues north (left) on the road.

4.3 – 4.8 –500 **(10)** Turn north (left) and descend at a steep angle for 0.5 mile until you reach the Rainbow Interconnect where the **road turns east (right) (13)**.

5

4.8 – 6.5   +250,–150 **(13)** Turn east (right) with the road and onto the Rainbow Interconnect, and follow the road for 1.7 miles until you reach the **junction (5)** of the Rainbow Interconnect and the High Loch Leven Lake marked trail.

6.5 – 7.7   –500 **(5)** Retrace your tracks and the High Loch Leven Lake tour for 1.2 miles until you reach the **starting point (1)**.

Winter trail

6   Lower Lola Montez Lake

MAP 3
PAGE 36

Difficulty	4
Length	6 miles round trip
Elevation	6600/+950,–950
Navigation	Road, map and compass
Time	Full day
Season	January through early April
USGS topo	7.5' series, Soda Springs
Start	Donner Summit Public Utility District office. Park on the south side of Interstate 80 at the Soda Springs exit; ask at the Donner Summit Lodge (and restaurant) for permission to use their parking lot. Walk north across the interstate, turn east (right) on the access road, and walk 0.1 mile to the east end of the PUD buildings where the road is no longer plowed.

Lower Lola Montez Lake is located among exposed granite cliffs where, by spring, creeks and waterfalls abound. These cliffs and the superb vistas to the south make this a wonderful tour for skiers with a good knowledge of navigating by map and compass.

All the lands between the interstate and the lake are private except for Section 8 in which the lake is located. The route described here, which begins at the interstate, follows a non-motorized public access route through the private lands.

Mileage Log

0.0 – 0.1   +50 **(1)** Ski northeast on the snow-covered road for 0.1 mile until you reach a **road junction (2)**.

0.1 – 1.0   +50,–200 **(2)** Turn northwest (left) and follow the road for 0.9 mile until you reach **Lower Castle Creek (3)** and the headwaters of the South Yuba River. After 0.1 mile you pass under power lines and after 0.5 mile you begin the descent to the creek.

> *Do not be intimidated by no trespassing signs just after turning onto this road. This road, or more accurately the trail it closely replaced, is a public access route open to non-motorized travel. But be aware that you must stay on the road, or trail where the road does not exist, until you reach Section 8 in which Lower Lola Montez Lake is located.*

1.0 – 1.5   +200 **(3)** Zig-zag northwest on the road for 0.5 mile until you reach a **fork in the road (4)**. The east (right) fork goes level for

34

a short distance to a house; do not take that fork. The tour continues on the west (left) fork that continues to climb.

1.5 – 2.2   +300 **(4)** Climb north on the west (left) fork for 0.7 mile until you reach a **drainage (6)**; the road disappears as the terrain levels near the drainage. One-tenth mile from the start of this section the topographic map shows a road junction (5); it was not visible when this tour was scouted.

2.2 – 2.9   +150 **(6)** Follow the drainage to the northwest, through jumbled terrain, for 0.7 mile until you reach a **large meadow (7)**.

2.9 – 3.2   +0 **(7)** Ski southwest for 0.3 mile until you reach **Lower Lola Montez Lake (8)**.

Exploring untracked snow   by Lee Griffith

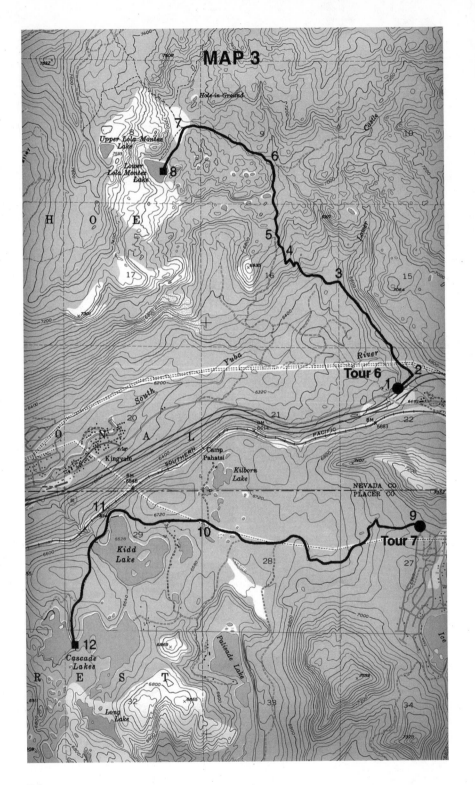

MAP 3

MAP 3
PAGE 36

Cascade Lakes **7**

Difficulty	2
Length	Up to 8 miles round trip
Elevation	7000/+700,–700
Navigation	Road
Time	Up to most of a day
Season	December through April
USGS topo	7.5′ series, Soda Springs
Start	End of Pahatsi Road. From Soda Springs drive 0.9 mile south on Soda Springs Road. Turn right onto Pahatsi Road and continue for 0.4 mile until it comes to a dead end at the entrance to Royal Gorge Cross Country Ski Resort. The tour begins here.

Cascade Lakes are located on a plateau, among many other lakes, in the Donner Summit area. There are fine views to the north from the vicinity of Kidd Lake.

This perfect cross-country skiing area is also the home of Royal Gorge Cross Country Ski Resort which charges for the use of their groomed trails on land they own or lease from private parties. If it were not for Pahatsi Road, a designated Public Travel Way, this area would be closed entirely to the non-paying public.

The route to Cascade Lakes, over the public route, is entirely on roads of which many are groomed for skiing by the resort or used by their Sno-Cats for access. In places where the public access road and the groomed tracks coincide, you may legally ski on the tracks.

Keep in mind that you must stay on the Public Travel Way that is marked with blue signs; return to it immediately if you accidentally wander off it. In the event you are approached by the resort's Nordic ski patrol, be pleasant to them, but be aware that they have no jurisdiction on the public road. Report any incidents of intimidation to the Forest Service in Truckee (916-587-3558).

Finally, you will probably find that the most difficult part of the tour to Cascade Lakes is locating a legal parking place.

Mileage Log

0.0 – 2.0 –300 **(9)** Ski west on unplowed Pahatsi Road for 2.0 miles until you reach the **sign across the road that marks the route to Royal Gorge's Wilderness Lodge (10)** at Kilborn Lake. In places where the public road and the Sno-Cat tracks or groomed trail cross or coincide, carefully follow the signs that mark the public road. You may find the following detailed description helpful in clarifying points of confusion.

7

From the starting point, ski a short distance west on Pahatsi Road, cross a groomed trail, continue west and encounter another groomed trail onto which you turn left. Ski for 25 yards, turn right off the groomed trail and continue west on the public road until you intersect a Sno-Cat track. Turn left onto the track and follow the marked public road to the sign across the road that marks the route to Royal Gorge's Wilderness Lodge.

2.0 – 2.8   –100 **(10)** Continue west on the public road for 0.8 mile until you reach the **dam (11)** at the north end of Kidd Lake. Do not follow the Sno-Cat track that leads to Royal Gorge's Wilderness Lodge.

2.8 – 3.8   +150,–150 **(11)** Continue south on the public road, past a second dam, over a small hill, and finally down for a total of 1.0 mile until you reach the **dam between upper and lower Cascade Lakes (12)**.

Northeast side of Basin Peak   by Dick Simpson

MAP 4
PAGE 40

Crows Nest 8

Difficulty	3
Length	5 miles round trip
Elevation	6850/+950,–950
Navigation	Map
Time	Most of a day
Season	Late December through mid-April
USGS topo	7.5′ series, Soda Springs, Norden
Start	End of Soda Springs Road, 2.3 miles south of Soda Springs. Parking is available at Serene Lake Lodge for a fee.

Although it is located in a heavily developed area, this is a very pleasant tour and over most of it you will feel very alone. The highlight of this tour is the view afforded the ridge, sometimes called Cornice Ridge, that overlooks Lake Van Norden — Crows Nest, Mount Judah, Castle Peak and more can be seen. Of course you can see back to Serene Lakes (Ice Lakes on maps) where you started the tour.

This tour does not actually go all the way to the summit of Crows Nest, but rather it stops at the base of its northwest ridge. Beyond here the terrain is not suitable for touring.

Mileage Log

0.0 – 0.4 +0 **(1)** Ski north along the east side of Serene Lakes (Ice Lakes) for 0.4 mile until you reach the summer **boat ramp (2)**.

0.4 – 0.7 +0 **(2)** Take off your skis and walk east on the subdivision road to the first intersection; turn left onto Lake Drive and walk to the next intersection; turn right onto Beacon Road and walk to Soda Springs Road for a total of 0.3 mile; and locate the **level, open area (3)** on the east side of Soda Springs Road opposite Donner Spitz 49.

0.7 – 1.2 +450 **(3)** Ski northeast through the level, open area (a public access route), cross a groomed Nordic trail, and climb northeast for a total of 0.5 mile until you reach the top of the **ridge (4)**.

1.2 – 1.8 –100 **(4)** Ski east along the ridge for 0.6 mile until you reach a broad **saddle (5)** and a groomed Nordic trail.

1.8 – 2.5 +400 **(5)** Cross the groomed trail and climb southeast for 0.7 mile until you reach the **base of Crows Nest (6)**.

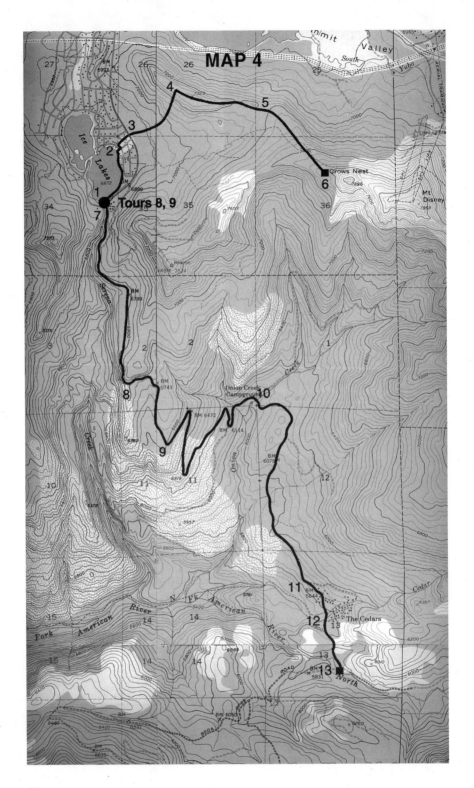

MAP 4
PAGE 40

The Cedars **9**

Difficulty	2 – 3
Length	Up to 13 miles round trip
Elevation	6850/Up to +1250,–1250
Navigation	Road
Time	Up to full day
Season	Late December through March
USGS topo	7.5′ series, Soda Springs, Norden, Granite Chief
Start	End of Soda Springs Road, 2.3 miles south of Soda Springs. Parking is available at Serene Lake Lodge, across the road from the starting point, for a fee.

If you pick a clear day with good snow conditions for this tour, you will be treated to an outstanding combination of good touring and spectacular scenery. This tour traverses steep canyon walls as it gradually but continuously descends more than 1000 feet down a road to the headwaters of the North Fork of the American River. Since there are excellent places to stop along the route, one requiring very little descent, you can shorten the tour without missing the beauty of the area.

Once you are down in the canyon, the thought of having to climb out may seem unappealing. Fortunately, if the conditions are good on your descent, there will be a nice track to ascend on the return. Also, the gradient is steady but never excessive.

Because this tour follows a narrow road with a steady gradient, save it for a time when the snow is soft, such as immediately after a light snowfall. Be aware of the potential avalanche danger in this area; exercise caution after heavy snowfalls or during other unstable conditions.

Mileage Log

0.0 – 1.4   –50 (7) Ski south on the snow-covered road for 1.4 miles until you reach a **small ridge (8)**. A Royal Gorge Cross Country Ski Resort groomed trail crosses the road on which you are skiing at 0.2 mile from the start. Stay on the marked public access route.

1.4 – 2.1   –200 (8) Descend on the road for 0.7 mile until you reach a **sharp left turn (9)**. Just off the road to the south is a large, open, flat area which is an excellent alternate destination and offers a breathtaking view. If you plan to ski farther, ski out to the rim overlooking the North Fork of the American River anyway. Snow Mountain (no. 2), the ascent of which is described separately in this guidebook, is prominent to the west with its steep cliffs descending into the "Royal Gorge." To the east, Mt. Lin-

9

coln, Anderson Peak and Tinker Knob form the ridge along which the Sugar Bowl to Squaw Valley tour (no. 12) traverses.

2.1 – 4.0   –550 **(9)** Return to the road if you have left it, and descend on the road for 1.9 miles as it zig-zags down until you reach the **bridge at Onion Creek (10)**. This is another good destination.

4.0 – 5.6   +50,–250 **(10)** Continue on the road for 1.6 miles, as it gradually climbs and then descends, until you reach a **road junction (11)**.

5.6 – 5.9   –50 **(11)** Take the south (right) fork and ski for 0.3 mile through the summer community of The Cedars until you reach **Cedar Creek (12)**.

5.9 – 6.3   +50,–50 **(12)** Be careful when crossing Cedar Creek and then continue on the road for 0.3 mile, always taking the right forks where there are choices, until you reach the bridge across the **North Fork of the American River (13)**.

Preparing for a quick descent

10 Mount Judah and Donner Peak

MAP 5A
PAGE 48

Difficulty	4
Length	3 miles round trip
Elevation	7050/+1350,−1350
Navigation	Map
Time	Half day
Season	Late December through early April
USGS topo	7.5′ series, Norden
Start	Alpine Skills Institute, 4.0 miles east of Interstate 80 and 0.2 mile east of Donner Ski Ranch on Donner Pass Road.

Many skiers climb Mount Judah and Donner Peak — some for the views and some for the excellent telemarking on the east side of the ridge formed by these two peaks. But the proximity of this tour to Alpine Skills Institute (ASI), which teaches mountaineering skills including backcountry ski techniques and offers inexpensive lodging, draws many of the skiers.

This tour affords superb views of nearby Mount Lincoln, Crows Nest and Anderson Peak, as well as Castle Peak and much more to the north. But all too often the ascent is made icy by strong winds. These same winds form cornices on the east side of the Mount Judah ridge.

Nevertheless, advanced skiers can thrill in the descent east from the Mount Judah ridge when snow in the bowl below is stable. Once down to the 7600-foot level, you can ascend the southeast shoulder of Donner Peak.

The Mount Judah Loop tour (no. 11) is an extension of this tour and includes a downhill run on a groomed slope at Sugar Bowl Ski Area.

Mileage Log

0.0 – 1.1 +1100 **(1)** Climb southeast on a ridge for 1.1 miles until you reach the **ridge (2)** of which Mount Judah is the high point.

1.1 – 1.5 +100 **(2)** Ski south along the ridge for 0.4 mile until you reach the **summit of Mount Judah (3)**.

1.5 – 2.2 −400 **(3)** Ski north along the ridge for 0.4 mile and then descend a ridge to the northeast for 0.3 mile until you reach the **saddle (4)** between Mount Judah and Donner Peak.

2.2 – 2.3 +150 **(4)** Climb northeast for 0.1 mile until you reach the **summit of Donner Peak (5)**.

2.3 – 2.4 −150 **(5)** Descend southwest for 0.1 mile until you reach the **saddle (4)** between Donner Peak and Mount Judah.

10

2.4 – 2.8   –200 **(5)** Descend west and then northwest for a total of 0.4 mile until you reach the **ridge (6)** that you ascended earlier.

2.8 – 3.4   –600 **(6)** Retrace your route for 0.6 mile until you reach the **starting point (1)**.

Windswept ridge on Sugar Bowl to Squaw Valley tour

11 Mount Judah Loop

Difficulty	4
Length	4 miles one-way
Elevation	7050/+1200,−1200
Navigation	Map
Time	Half day
Season	Late December through early April
USGS topo	7.5′ series, Norden
Start	Alpine Skills Institute, 4.0 miles east of Interstate 80 and 0.2 mile east of Donner Ski Ranch on Donner Pass Road.
End	Donner Ski Ranch, 3.8 miles east of Interstate 80 on Donner Pass Road and 0.2 mile west of Alpine Skills Institute.

This loop offers all the features of the Mount Judah and Donner Peak tour (no. 10), superb views and opportunities to enjoy some telemarking, plus a more moderate descent which includes a run down one of Sugar Bowl Ski Area's groomed slopes. Refer to the Mount Judah and Donner Peak tour for more details about safety and skiing in this area.

Mileage Log

0.0 – 0.6   +600 **(1)** Climb southeast on a ridge for 0.6 mile until you reach a **more level area (6)**.

0.6 – 1.0   +200 **(6)** Climb southeast and then east for a total of 0.4 mile until you reach the saddle **(4)** between Mount Judah and Donner Peak. It is a short climb to the summit of Donner Peak from the saddle.

1.0 – 1.7   +400 **(4)** Climb southwest up a ridge for 0.3 mile until you reach a billboard-like structure and then ski south along the ridge for 0.4 mile until you reach the **summit of Mount Judah (3)**.

1.7 – 2.1   −400 **(3)** Descend southwest along the ridge for 0.4 mile until you reach a **saddle (7)**, often referred to as Rolling Pass, and intersect the ski area groomed trail. This section contains open, lightly forested, and densely wooded areas. At one point you will encounter a rock outcropping. Unless cornices prevent you, ski around the outcropping on its east (left) side.

2.1 – 2.5   −350 **(7)** Descend on the groomed ski run to the northwest for 0.4 mile until you reach a **cafe (8)**.

2.5 – 3.5   −450 **(8)** Leave the groomed ski run and ski north, losing elevation slowly, for 1.0 mile until you reach the south end of **Lake**

11

Mary (9). Current expansion plans for Sugar Bowl Ski Area call for new ski runs to cross this section of the tour.

3.5 – 3.7 +0 **(9)** Ski north across Lake Mary and and then continue north for a total of 0.2 mile until you reach **Donner Ski Ranch (10)**. It is a short walk back to the starting point.

Benson Hut   by Tom McNicholas

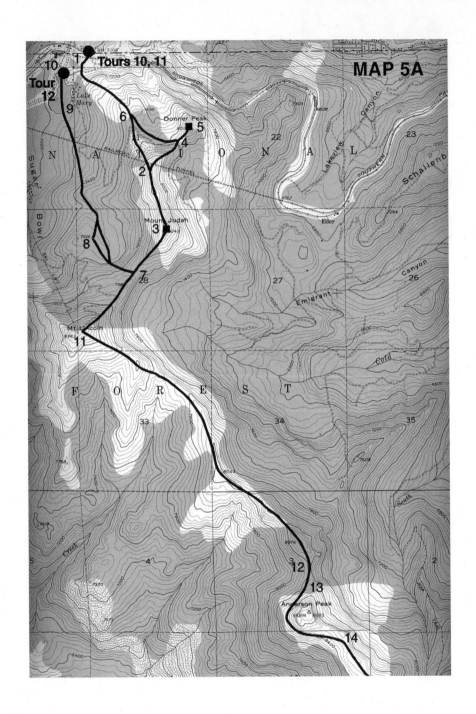

MAP 5A

Tours 10, 11

Tour 12

48

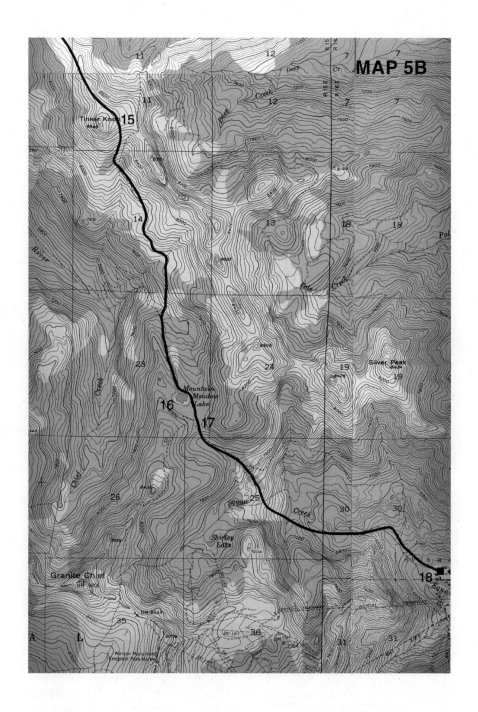

12 Sugar Bowl to Squaw Valley

Difficulty	5
Length	11 miles one-way
Elevation	7050/+2550,−3300
Navigation	Map and compass
Time	Very long day
Season	Late January through early April
USGS topo	7.5′ series, Norden, Granite Chief, Tahoe City
Start	Donner Ski Ranch, 3.8 miles east of Interstate 80 on Donner Pass Road.
End	Squaw Valley Ski Area on the west side of Highway 89, 9.1 miles south of Interstate 80 and 5.4 miles north of Tahoe City

The tour from Sugar Bowl to Squaw Valley is a classic in the North Tahoe area. A large elevation gain and loss, a spectacular traverse of the windswept and corniced ridge between Mt. Lincoln and Anderson Peak, potentially poor snow conditions, and considerable navigation all contribute to the challenge of this tour. This tour is much more difficult than its 11-mile length indicate and should only be attempted during periods of good weather.

This tour crosses two ski resorts, Sugar Bowl and Squaw Valley. Avoid their groomed slopes when possible and exercise caution when crossing them.

Mileage Log

At Donner Ski Ranch, the starting point, you have an excellent view of the route to the summit of Mt. Lincoln which is 1350 feet above.

0.0 – 0.2 +0 **(10)** Ski south for 0.2 mile until you reach the south end of **Lake Mary (9)**.

0.2 – 1.6 +800 **(9)** Traverse and climb south and then southeast for a total of 1.4 miles until you reach a **saddle (7)**, often referred to as Rolling Pass, on the northeast ridge of Mt. Lincoln. If you stay low you may pass by a cafe (8) that is part of Sugar Bowl Ski Area. Current expansion plans for Sugar Bowl Ski Area call for new ski runs to cross this section of the tour. You will be permitted to cross them.

1.6 – 2.2 +550 **(7)** Climb southwest on the ridge for 0.6 mile until you reach the **summit of Mt. Lincoln (11)**. As you approach Mt. Lincoln, do not attempt to ski the east bowl of the mountain; the avalanche danger is extreme.

2.2 – 4.7 +650,−850 **(11)** Ski southeast along the ridge for 2.5 miles until you reach the **saddle (12)** north of Anderson Peak. Make sure that no downhill skiers follow when you descend from Mt. Lincoln. Also, be aware that this section of ridge is often heavily corniced on its northeast side.

4.7 – 4.8 +50 **(12)** Ski 0.1 mile south until you reach **Benson Hut (13)**. You can obtain current information about reservations for this Sierra Club hut by contacting:

> Clair Tappaan Lodge
> P.O. Box 36
> Norden, California 95724
> (916) 426-3632

4.8 – 5.6 +250 **(13)** Ski and climb 0.8 mile around the west side of Anderson Peak until you reach the **ridge (14)** between Anderson Peak and Tinker Knob.

5.6 – 6.6 +200 **(14)** Ski southeast for 1.0 mile along the ridge until you reach the **east side of Tinker Knob (15)**.

6.6 – 8.8 –800 **(15)** Ski south and descend 500 feet (be careful not to lose too much elevation); then leave the drainage you have been following and traverse south, below and to the west of a ridge, for a total of 2.2 miles until you reach **Mountain Meadow Lake (16)**.

8.8 – 9.0 +50 **(16)** Ski 0.2 mile south until you reach a broad **saddle (17)** where you can see Squaw Valley below.

9.0 – 11.3 –1650 **(17)** Descend a total of 2.3 miles, first southeast to Squaw Creek and Shirley Canyon, then down Shirley Canyon to **Squaw Valley (18)**. Be careful to stay clear of any avalanche paths along Squaw Creek.

13 Lakes Crossing

MAP 6
PAGE 53

Difficulty	3
Length	3 miles one-way
Elevation	7200/+50,–200
Navigation	Map
Time	Half day
Season	Late December through mid-April
USGS topo	7.5' series, Norden
Start	East end of the Donner Pass SnoPark on Interstate 80. Exit the highway at Castle Peak Area and Boreal Ridge. Drive east on the south frontage road for 0.2 mile to the SnoPark.
End	Donner Ski Ranch, 3.8 miles east of Interstate 80 on Donner Pass Road.

The Lakes Crossing from Interstate 80 to Old Highway 40 rolls across relatively level terrain. Although technically not difficult, navigating efficiently can be a little troublesome due to the many little features that break up straight-forward progress. Hopefully this tour description will eliminate that problem.

The ideal scenario combines this tour with the Donner Pass Road to Interstate 80 via Boreal Ridge tour (no. 14). The two form a wonderful loop.

Mileage Log

0.0 – 0.2 +0 **(1)** Ski east for 0.2 mile until you are adjacent to the **rest area (2)** on the south side of the interstate.

0.2 – 0.6 +0 **(2)** Ski east and parallel to the interstate for 0.4 mile until your reach an **open area (3)**.

0.6 – 1.4 +50,–50 **(3)** Ski southeast for 0.5 mile until you reach Azalea Lake and another 0.3 mile until you reach **Flora Lake (4)**. A rock wall on the southwest side of Flora Lake is very obvious. It is a short distance to the top of a small rise east of Flora Lake and a wonderful view east of Donner Lake, the interstate and the transcontinental railroad — a great place for lunch. Donner Peak is visible to the south too.

1.4 – 1.9 +0 **(4)** Ski south, picking the best route around little obstacles, for 0.5 mile until you reach **Lake Angela (5)**.

1.9 – 2.5 –150 **(5)** Ski along Angela Lake for 0.2 mile to the dam and then descend south for 0.4 mile until you reach **Donner Pass Road (6)**. It is not necessary to descend to the plowed road if you are combining this tour with the Donner Pass Road to Interstate 80 via Boreal Ridge tour. Simply loop around from below the dam to Donner Ski Ranch.

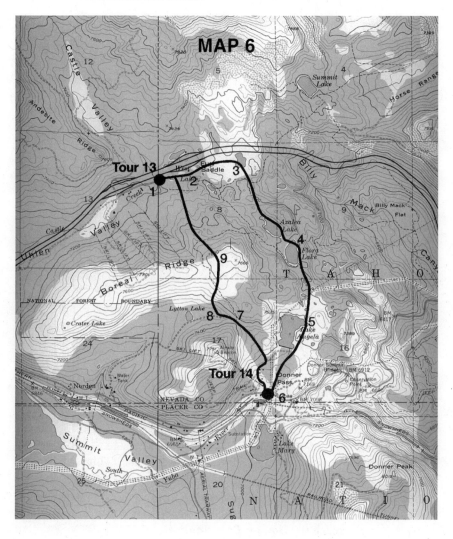

MAP 6
PAGE 53

14 Donner Pass Road to Interstate 80 via Boreal Ridge

Difficulty	4
Length	2 miles one-way
Elevation	7050/+650,–500
Navigation	Map
Time	Half day
Season	Late December through mid-April
USGS topo	7.5' series, Norden
Start	Donner Ski Ranch, 3.8 miles east of Interstate 80 on Donner Pass Road.
End	East end of the Donner Pass SnoPark on Interstate 80. Exit the interstate at Castle Peak Area and Boreal Ridge. Drive east on the south frontage road for 0.2 mile to the SnoPark.

You may choose this tour to enjoy the downhill run from Boreal Ridge through powder that is often found on the north-facing side of the ridge. But more of you will choose it in order to create a loop in combination with the Lakes Crossing tour (no. 13).

Mileage Log

0.0 – 0.7   +350 **(6)** Climb north, staying near the east (right) edge of the groomed ski run, for 0.7 mile until you reach the **saddle (7)** to the northeast of Peak 7751.

0.7 – 0.9   –100 **(7)** Descend northwest for 0.2 mile until you reach the base of a **chairlift (8)**.

0.9 – 1.3   +300 **(8)** Climb north for 0.4 mile until you reach the top, **east end of Boreal Ridge (9)**. You are too far west if you encounter the groomed, downhill slopes of Boreal Ridge Ski Area on the north side of the ridge; ski east to avoid these slopes.

1.3 – 2.1   –400 **(9)** Descend north through moderately forested terrain for 0.7 mile until you are near the highway, and then ski parallel to the highway, this could be either east (right) or west (left), until you reach the **Donner Pass SnoPark (1)**.

MAP 7
PAGE 57

Andesite Peak **15**

Difficulty	3
Length	5 miles round trip
Elevation	7200/+1000,−1000
Navigation	Road and map
Time	Half day
Season	December through mid-April
USGS topo	7.5′ series, Norden
Start	The plowed loading zone on the north side of Interstate 80 at the Castle Peak Area and Boreal Ridge exit. Parking is available at the SnoPark located at the east end of the frontage road which is located on the south side of the interstate.

The tour to Andesite Peak, along the west side of Andesite Ridge, is an excellent alternative to the popular tour up Castle Valley to Round Valley and Peter Grubb Hut (nos. 17 and 18). The Andesite Ridge Loop tour (no. 16) describes a loop that combines this tour with those. All the tours in this area feature magnificent scenery, but the tour to Andesite Peak also offers a snack or lunch on its dramatic summit.

Mileage Log

0.0 – 0.2 +100 **(1)** Ski 0.1 mile east on the road which parallels the interstate, and then ski 0.1 mile northwest on the same road until you reach a **road junction (2)**. The road continuing northwest (straight) leads to Castle Valley while this tour follows the road to the west (left).

0.2 – 0.4 +100 **(2)** Turn west (left) and follow the road for 0.2 mile until you reach a **road junction (3)**.

0.4 – 0.9 +100 **(3)** Take the north (right) fork and ski for 0.5 mile until you reach a **meadow (4)** on the southwest (left) side of the road. Shortly before reaching the meadow you pass a gently sloping, open area to the northeast which is ideal for playing and practicing technique.

0.9 – 1.9 +350 **(4)** Continue on the road for 1.0 mile until you reach the **west ridge of Andesite Peak (5)**. Take the north or east (right) fork at all junctions you encounter.

1.9 – 2.3 +350 **(5)** Climb west, picking the easiest route, for 0.4 mile until you reach the **summit of Andesite Peak (6)**.

MAP 7
PAGE 57

16 Andesite Ridge Loop

Difficulty	3
Length	4 miles round trip
Elevation	7200/+700,–700
Navigation	Road, marked trail and map
Time	Half day
Season	December through mid-April
USGS topo	7.5′ series, Norden
Start	The plowed loading zone on the north side of Interstate 80 at the Castle Peak Area and Boreal Ridge exit. Parking is available at the SnoPark located at the east end of the frontage road which is located on the south side of the interstate.

Here is a wonderful loop trip that combines some of the best that the Castle Valley area has to offer. A short side trip to the summit of Andesite Peak (no. 15) can be added and a side trip to Round Valley and Peter Grubb Hut (no. 18) can be added to make it a full day of skiing.

Mileage Log

0.0 – 1.9   +650 **(1)** Follow the Andesite Peak tour (no. 15) for 1.9 miles until you reach the **west ridge of Andesite Peak (5)**. The peak can easily be ascended from the here.

1.9 – 2.7   +50 **(5)** Continue northeast on the road and continue to traverse after it ends for a total of 0.8 mile until you reach **Castle Pass (7)**. Do not follow any road that descends to the west.

2.7 – 2.8   –100 **(7)** Descend the steep slope to the east (right) of Castle Pass for 0.1 mile until you reach a **flat area (8)**.

2.8 – 4.2   –500 **(8)** Ski southeast on a road for 1.4 miles until you reach the **road junction (2)** that you encountered earlier in the tour. The road you are descending can be difficult to recognize, and the trail markers are far apart and few due to the sparse vegetation. However, it is hard to go wrong if you simply parallel Andesite Ridge.

4.2 – 4.4   –100 **(2)** Retrace your tracks for 0.2 mile until you reach the **starting point (1)**.

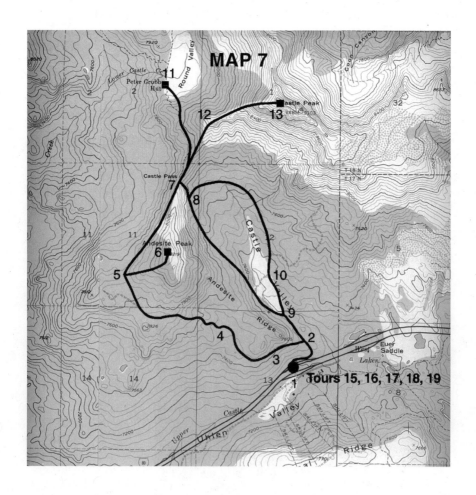

MAP 7

Tours 15, 16, 17, 18, 19

17 Castle Valley Loop

MAP 7
PAGE 57

Difficulty	2
Length	4 miles round trip
Elevation	7200/+600,–600
Navigation	Road, marked trail and map
Time	Few hours
Season	December through early April
USGS topo	7.5′ series, Norden
Start	The plowed loading zone on the north side of Interstate 80 at the Castle Peak Area and Boreal Ridge exit. Parking is available at the SnoPark located at the east end of the frontage road which is located on the south side of the interstate.

The loop through Castle Valley combines a straight forward ski on a road to the base of Castle Pass with a return trip through woods. While the entire tour has been marked with blue diamonds, the markers are far between in the sparsely wooded areas and hard to follow in the moderately heavy wooded areas. Nevertheless, the loop is easy to make because it simply circles the valley.

The loop is described in a clockwise direction. In this way you ascend on the heavily used road and descend on the little used forested section. The loop can be combined with any of several other tours in the area.

Mileage Log

0.0 – 0.2 +100 (1) Ski 0.1 mile east on the road which parallels the interstate, and then ski 0.1 mile northwest on the same road until you reach a **road junction (2)**. This tour continues northwest (straight) on the road while the road to the west (left) loops around the west side of Andesite Peak (nos. 15 and 16).

0.2 – 0.4 +0 (2) Ski northwest (straight) on the road for 0.2 mile until you reach the edge of the **meadow (9)** in Castle Valley.

0.4 – 1.6 +500 (9) Ski northwest on the road, which may be difficult to discern, for 1.2 miles until you reach the **flat area (8)** at the base of Castle Pass.

1.6 – 2.8 –450 (8) Traverse and gradually loose elevation as you loop clockwise through the woods for 1.2 miles until you exit the woods and reach the **meadow (10)** in Castle Valley.

2.8 – 3.1 –50 (10) Ski south along the east side of the meadow for 0.3 mile until you reach the **road (9)** you skied earlier.

3.1 – 3.5   –100 **(9)** Turn southeast (left) onto the road and retrace your tracks for 0.4 mile until you reach the **starting point (1)**.

Okay, which way now?   by Clara Yen

MAP 7
PAGE 57

18 Round Valley and Peter Grubb Hut

Difficulty	3
Length	5 miles round trip
Elevation	7200/+1000,–1000
Navigation	Road, marked trail and map
Time	Half day
Season	December through April
USGS topo	7.5′ series, Norden
Start	The plowed loading zone on the north side of Interstate 80 at the Castle Peak Area and Boreal Ridge exit. Parking is available at the SnoPark located at the east end of the frontage road which is located on the south side of the interstate.

Peter Grubb Hut, built by the Sierra Club in the thirties, is a popular destination for ski tourers. Located in Round Valley, the hut is often used to make the five-mile round trip tour into an overnight trip. To use this Sierra Club hut, make reservations well in advance by contacting:

> Clair Tappaan Lodge
> P.O. Box 36
> Norden, California 95724
> (916) 426-3632

Nearby Castle Peak (no. 19), Basin Peak, and the ridge between the two peaks are popular destinations for those with sufficient time to explore. The less adventuresome can enjoy the more mellow terrain of Round Valley itself.

Mileage Log

0.0 – 0.2 +100 **(1)** Ski 0.1 mile east on the road which parallels the interstate, and then ski 0.1 mile northwest on the same road until you reach a **road junction (2)**. This tour continues northwest (straight) on the road while the road to the west (left) loops around the west side of Andesite Ridge (nos. 15 and 16).

0.2 – 0.4 +0 **(2)** Ski northwest (straight) on the road for 0.2 mile until you reach the edge of the **meadow (9)** in Castle Valley.

0.4 – 1.6 +500 **(9)** Ski northwest on the road, which may be difficult to discern, for 1.2 miles until you reach the **flat area (8)** at the base of Castle Pass.

1.6 – 1.7 +100 **(8)** Climb 0.1 mile northwest until you reach **Castle Pass (7)**.

1.7 – 2.5 +100,–200 **(7)** Ski north while traversing the west ridge of Castle Peak for 0.5 mile and then descend 0.3 mile until you reach **Round Valley and Peter Grubb Hut (11)**. In very heavy winters, most or all of Peter Grubb Hut is covered by snow.

Peter Grubb Hut   by Dick Simpson

19 Castle Peak

MAP 7
PAGE 57

Difficulty	4
Length	5 miles round trip
Elevation	7200/+1900,–1900
Navigation	Road, marked trail and map
Time	Most of a day
Season	December through April
USGS topo	7.5' series, Norden
Start	The plowed loading zone on the north side of Interstate 80 at the Castle Peak Area and Boreal Ridge exit. Parking is available at the SnoPark located at the east end of the frontage road which is located on the south side of the interstate.

Viewed from the south, it is clear why Castle Peak was named. A massive fortress, Castle Peak stands alone (except for Basin Peak) commanding an awe inspiring view.

The summit has long been a destination for skiers in the Donner Pass area. In addition to the scenery, the bowl to the west of the summit attracts telemark skiers. Be aware that this bowl and many of the slopes in the vicinity are unsafe when unstable snow conditions prevail.

Mileage Log

0.0 – 1.7 +700 **(1)** Follow the Round Valley and Peter Grubb Hut tour (no. 18) for 1.7 miles until you reach **Castle Pass (7)**.

1.7 – 2.2 +350 **(7)** Ski north for 0.5 mile until you reach the **ridge (12)** that leads to the summit of Castle Peak.

2.2 – 2.7 +850 **(12)** Ski east on the ridge for 0.5 mile until you reach the **summit of Castle Peak (13)**.

Donner Pass to Highway 89 via Mt. Lola 20

Difficulty	5
Length	19 miles one-way
Elevation	7200/+3000,−3800
Navigation	Road, map and compass
Time	Very long day
Season	Late December through early April
USGS topo	7.5′ series, Norden, Independence Lake, Weber Peak, Sierraville
Start	The plowed loading zone on the north side of Interstate 80 at the Castle Peak Area and Boreal Ridge exit. Parking is available at the SnoPark located at the east end of the frontage road which is located on the south side of the interstate.
End	Junction of Henness Pass-Jackson Meadows Road and Highway 89, 15 miles north of Interstate 80.

Don't miss this tour if you have the skills and stamina to do it. This tour covers a multitude of terrain as it weaves from Castle Valley to Round Valley to Paradise Valley and then climaxes with the ascent of Mt. Lola which commands a spectacular panorama. Once on the summit, you still have an exciting 2700-foot descent to the Little Truckee River.

Since the length and the route-finding are challenging, only very competent backcountry travelers should attempt this tour. You can ski this tour in a single day when the days are long and the snow is well-consolidated, such as in early spring. If you intend to do this tour earlier, such as in mid-winter, expect to spend at least one night snow-camping.

Mileage Log

0.0 – 2.5 +800,−200 **(1)** Follow the Round Valley and Peter Grubb Hut tour (no. 18) for 2.5 miles until you reach **Peter Grubb Hut (2)**. In this section you ski through Castle Valley, cross Castle Pass, and descend into Round Valley.

2.5 – 4.3 +450,−350 **(2)** Climb north past Basin Peak and then descend for a total of 1.8 miles until you reach the broad, **northwest shoulder of Basin Peak (3)**.

4.3 – 5.0 −350 **(3)** Descend along the broad shoulder until the terrain to the north looks moderate; then turn north and drop down for a total of 0.7 mile until you reach **Paradise Valley (4)**. Paradise Valley is wooded but not dense enough to obscure the view to the northwest where the tour continues.

20

5.0 – 6.8   +250 **(4)** Traverse and climb to the west, turn northeast as you round a ridge, and traverse for a total of 1.8 miles until you reach **White Rock Lake (5)**. You can avoid having to climb up to the lake along White Rock Creek by maintaining a level traverse at the 7800-foot level as you ski northeast.

6.8 – 7.6   +600 **(5)** Ascend northeast for 0.8 mile until you reach **Peak 8388 (6)**.

7.6 – 8.6   +850,–100 **(6)** Descend east from the peak and then ascend northeast at a very steep angle along a narrow ridge for a total of 1.0 mile until you reach the **summit of Mt. Lola (7)**. In this section, be aware of small but potentially dangerous cornices. If you are doing this tour in a single day, don't get too cocky once on the summit — you have not yet covered half the miles. Fortunately, the remainder of the trip is either downhill or level. So take time to enjoy the outstanding view.

The next challenge is to drop down to Cold Stream which you follow north. Be wary of dropping directly from the summit of Mt. Lola into the drainage — there may be a cornice to the northeast.

8.6 – 10.6 –1450 **(7)** Ski north along the ridge from the summit of Mt. Lola until you can safely drop down into the bowl to the east; drop down into the bowl and continue by descending northeast down Cold Stream for a total of 2.0 miles until you reach **Cold Stream Meadow (8)**.

10.6 – 12.3 –300 **(8)** Continue down Cold Stream, locate the road as you descend, and continue on the road for a total of 1.7 miles until you reach a **road junction (9)**. In the event that you do not find the road as you descend, stop descending when you reach the location where the Cold Stream drainage narrows and drops abruptly ahead; turn east (right) and ski a short distance until you reach the road.

12.3 – 14.2 –800 **(9)** At the road junction turn north (left) and descend on the road for 1.9 miles until you reach **Henness Pass Road (10)**.

14.2 – 17.1 +50,–200 **(10)** Turn east (right) onto Henness Pass Road and follow it for 2.9 miles until you reach a **road junction (11)**.

17.1 – 17.8 +0 **(11)** Turn west (left) and follow the road until you reach the bridge across the Little Truckee River and then continue a short distance for a total of 0.7 mile until you reach **Henness Pass-Jackson Meadows Road (12)**.

20

17.8 – 19.3 –50 **(12)** Turn east (right) onto and follow Henness Pass-Jackson Meadows Road for 1.5 miles until you reach **Highway 89 (13)**.

Fresh powder snow near Round Valley   by Dick Simpson

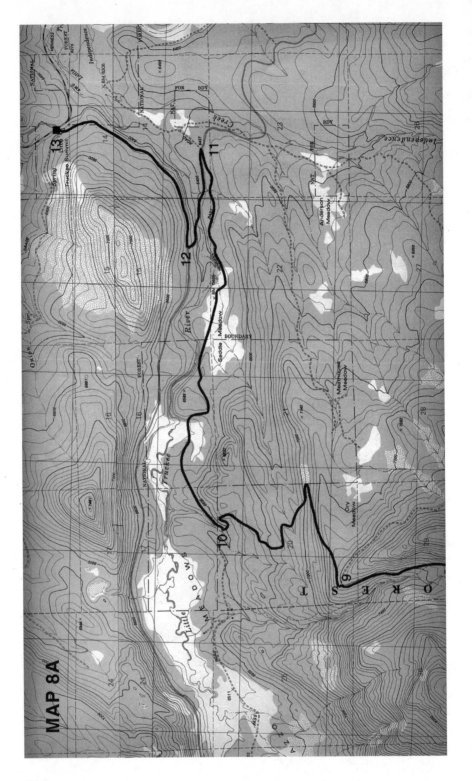

MAP 8A

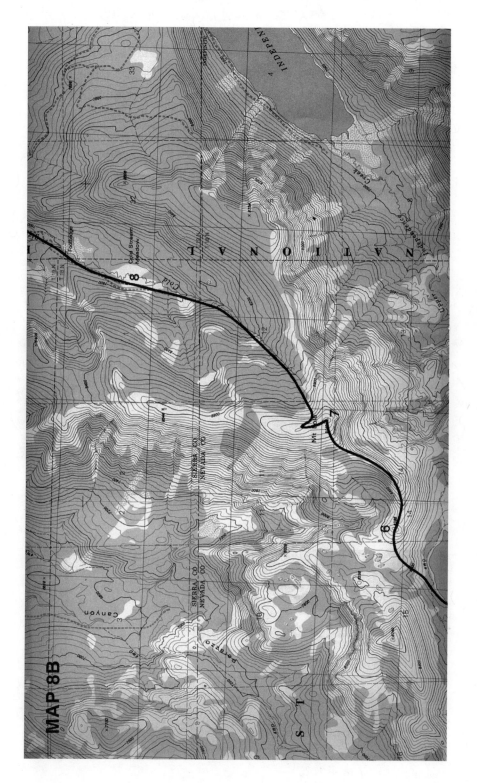

MAP 8B

67

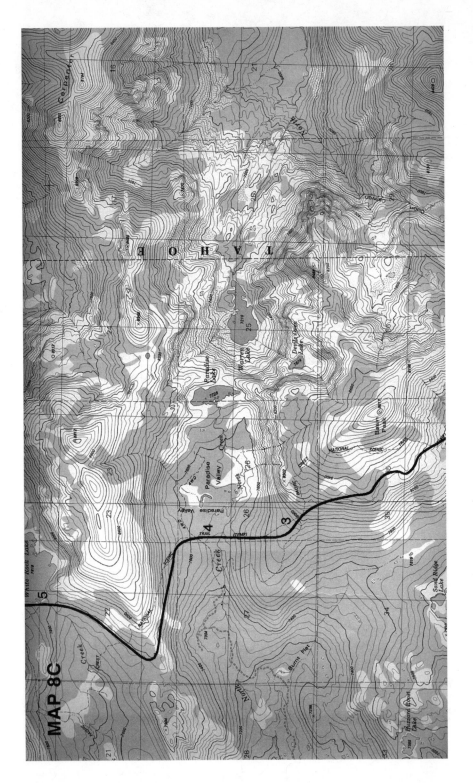

MAP 8C

68

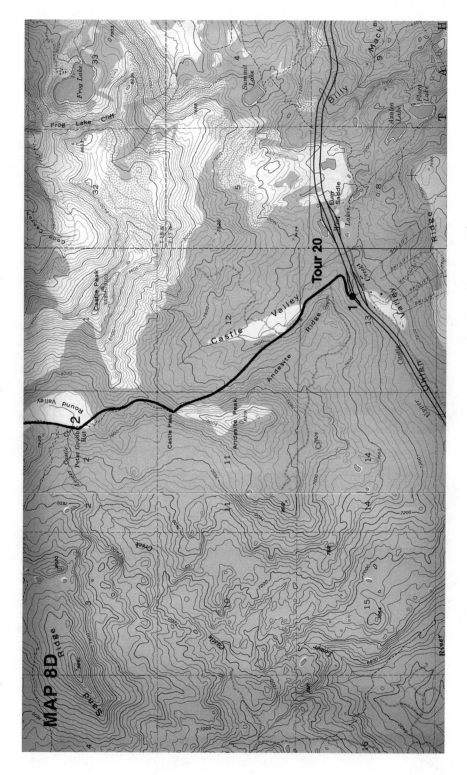

MAP 8D

21 Summit Lake

MAP 9

PAGE 71

Difficulty	2 – 3
Length	Up to 4 miles round trip
Elevation	7200/Up to +400,–400
Navigation	Map
Time	Up to half day
Season	Late December through mid-April
USGS topo	7.5′ series, Norden
Start	The plowed loading zone on the north side of Interstate 80 at the Castle Peak Area and Boreal Ridge exit. Parking is available at the SnoPark located at the east end of the frontage road which is located on the south side of the interstate.

You will find excellent touring terrain to the north of Interstate 80 between the starting point and Summit Lake. This mostly open, rolling terrain is an ideal place to enjoy an afternoon. Nearby slopes can provide hours of pleasurable telemark practice. There are countless spots to enjoy a lunch with a dramatic view.

Surprisingly, unlike its neighboring tours to Castle Valley and Round Valley (nos. 17 and 18), the area covered in this tour to Summit Lake is much less traveled. In fact, even when traveled by others, you can find an untracked route since there is no single, distinct one.

A couple words of caution. The first part of the tour, after leaving the snow-covered road, can be plagued by many small rocky gullies if there is insufficient snow. Also, finding Summit Lake, hidden within dense timber, is not a simple task.

Mileage Log

0.0 – 0.1 +50 **(1)** Ski 0.1 mile east on the road which parallels the interstate until you reach the location where the **road turns northwest (left) (2)**.

Leave the road and explore to the northeast at your leisure or continue to Summit Lake as described below.

0.1 – 1.7 +250,–100 **(2)** Leave the road and ski northeast for 1.6 miles to **Summit Lake (3)**. You will need to use a map because there are no markers or roads to follow. You may find it necessary to climb up above the trees to spot Summit Lake.

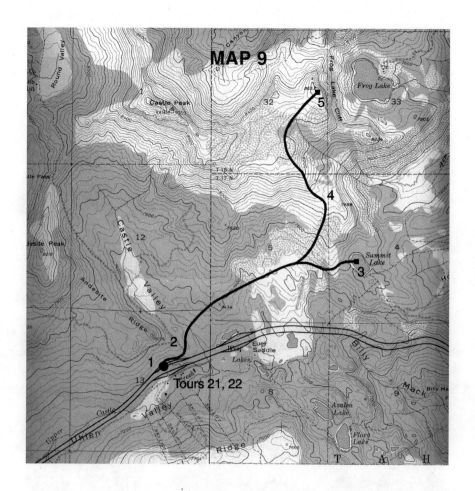

MAP 9

Tours 21, 22

Getting to the start is the biggest challenge   by Michael Snodgrass

72

MAP 9
PAGE 71

Frog Lake Cliff 22

Difficulty	4
Length	5 miles round trip
Elevation	7200/+1400,–1400
Navigation	Map
Time	Most of a day
Season	Late December through mid-April
USGS topo	7.5′ series, Norden
Start	The plowed loading zone on the north side of Interstate 80 at the Castle Peak Area and Boreal Ridge exit. Parking is available at the SnoPark located at the east end of the frontage road which is located on the south side of the interstate.

The top of a vertical cliff, plummeting more than 1000 feet straight down to Frog Lake below, is the destination of this tour. All the while you are climbing, you have an unobstructed view to the south. From the top the view to the east is marvelous.

But many skiers will choose this tour simply for the return descent — 1000 feet of uninterrupted slopes just begging to be carved. However, powder snow will not linger on this south-facing slope and the descent is best left for spring-like conditions. You should also exercise caution when choosing this tour — it should never be attempted when the snow is unstable.

Mileage Log

0.0 – 0.1 +50 (1) Ski 0.1 mile east on the road which parallels the interstate until you reach the location where the **road turns northwest (left) (2)**.

0.1 – 1.8 +550 (2) Leave the road and climb gradually northeast for 1.7 miles until you reach a **ridge (4)** to the north of Summit Lake.

1.8 – 2.7 +800 (4) Climb northwest on the ridge and then northeast above a drainage for a total of 0.9 mile until you reach **Frog Lake Cliff (5)**. Exercise caution near the cliff.

23 Donner Memorial State Park

MAP 10
PAGE 75

Difficulty	1
Length	2 miles round trip
Elevation	5950/Nil
Navigation	Road and marked trail
Time	Few hours
Season	Late December through March
USGS topo	7.5′ series, Truckee, Norden
Start	The SnoPark at Donner Memorial State Park which is located at the east end of Donner Lake. Walk to the entrance building of the campground (closed in winter) and the trailhead is located just beyond.

Donner Memorial State Park is a perfect place to enjoy a few hours on a winter afternoon. The tour is level, well-marked, and popular among beginners. While you are there, you can also visit the park museum and learn the saga of California pioneers.

Mileage Log

0.0 – 0.0 +0 **(1)** Ski downhill on a road for 25 yards until you reach Donner Creek, cross the creek on a bridge, and continue for another 25 yards until you reach a **fork in the road (1)**.

0.0 – 1.1 +0 **(1)** Follow the west (right) fork and ski for 1.1 miles along the south shore of Donner Lake until you reach **China Cove (2)**. Here a marker indicates the point where the ski touring trail leaves the road. You can lengthen this tour by skiing along the south shore of Donner Lake west of China Cove and then returning to complete the standard tour. However, do not ski on the lake itself — it is never stable.

1.1 – 1.6 +0 **(2)** Follow the marked trail east (left) for 0.5 mile until you reach a snow-covered **road (3)**.

1.6 – 2.0 +0 **(3)** Ski east on the road for 0.4 mile until you reach the location where the **road turns north (4)**.

2.0 – 2.3 +0 **(4)** Ski north on the road for 0.3 mile until you reach Donner Creek and the **ending point (1)**.

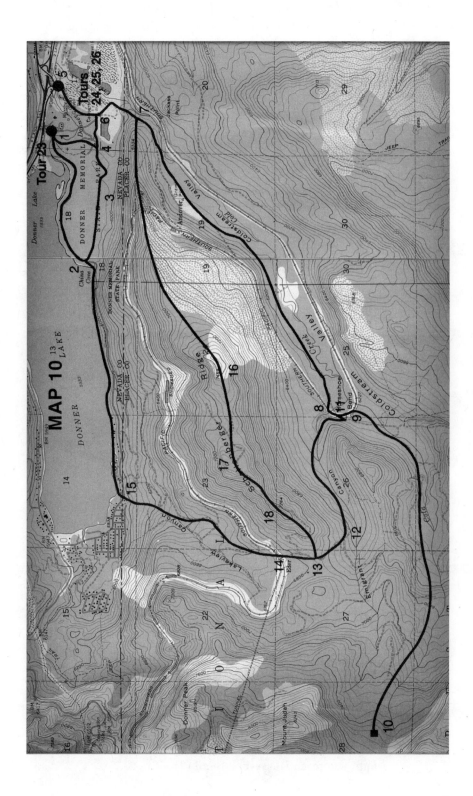

24 Coldstream Valley

MAP 10
PAGE 75

Difficulty	2 – 4
Length	Up to 12 miles round trip
Elevation	5950/Up to +1550,–1550
Navigation	Road and map
Time	Up to full day
Season	Late December through March
USGS topo	7.5′ series, Truckee, Norden
Start	The entrance to the gravel pit just south of Interstate 80 where Donner Pass Road crosses it. This is located just south of two gas stations.

This tour takes you through historically rich Coldstream Valley, over a beautiful section of the Emigrant Trail on which pioneers crossed the Sierra Nevada in search of gold and a new life, and alongside railroad tracks laid over 100 years ago as part of the transcontinental railroad. This era is captured at nearby Donner Memorial State Park museum.

Skiers of all abilities can enjoy a tour through Coldstream Valley. The first three-and-one-half miles climb only 300 feet to Horseshoe Bend. Advancing beginners can ski as far as they desire and then retrace their tracks. More advanced skiers can continue up Cold Creek to the bowl below Mt. Lincoln. The corniced ridge above the bowl is visible as you ski through Coldstream Valley.

Keep in mind when planning to tour here that the starting elevation is very low and the tour may be a poor choice in periods of low snowfall.

Two other tours in the area, the Schallenberger Loop tour (no. 25) and the Schallenberger Ridge tour (no. 26), make loops that include this tour.

Mileage Log

0.0 – 0.4 +0 **(5)** Ski south on the road for 0.4 mile until you reach a **road junction (6)**. This section may be plowed in times of low snow.

0.4 – 0.7 +100 **(6)** Ski on the east (left) fork until the road begins to climb, then climb at a steep angle for a total of 0.3 mile until you reach the location where the **road levels (7)**.

0.7 – 3.3 +200 **(7)** Follow the level road as it continues up the valley for 2.6 miles until you reach the **railroad tracks (8)** where the road seems to disappear.

> *You may not intersect the railroad tracks at the exact location shown on the map. If not, you must modify the directions appropriately.*

3.3 – 3.5 +0 **(8)** Ski south (left) alongside the railroad tracks for 0.2 mile until you reach **Horseshoe Bend (9)**.

3.5 – 6.2   +1250 **(9)** Leave the railroad tracks, and ski southwest and then west up Cold Creek for a total of 2.7 miles until you reach the **bowl (10)** below Mt. Lincoln. Do not expect to follow the road in this section. The bowl is a major avalanche hazard — do not climb up it or enter parts that may be unsafe.

It's great to be high!

Difficulty	4
Length	6 miles one-way or
	10 miles round trip
Elevation	5950/+900,−850 one-way or
	5950/+900,−900 round trip
Navigation	Road and map one-way or
	road, marked trail and map round trip
Time	Full day
Season	January through March
USGS topo	7.5′ series, Truckee, Norden
Start	The entrance to the gravel pit just south of Interstate 80 where Donner Pass Road crosses it. This is located just south of two gas stations.
End	Southwest end of Donner Lake on or near South Shore Drive about 0.7 mile south of Donner Pass Road. A street map may be useful in locating your car at the conclusion of the tour if you park on other than South Shore Drive. It is also possible to end the tour at the starting point.

This tour loops around Schallenberger Ridge by combining an easy tour up Coldstream Valley with more challenging skiing in Emigrant and Lakeview canyons. The most difficult section is the final descent through the dense trees of Lakeview Canyon to Donner Lake.

Mileage Log

0.0 – 3.3   +300 **(5)** Follow the Coldstream Valley tour (no. 24) for 3.3 miles until you reach the **railroad tracks (8)**.

You may not intersect the railroad tracks at the exact location shown on the map. If not, you must modify the directions appropriately.

3.3 – 3.4   +0 **(8)** Ski south (left) along side the railroad tracks, cross the creek that drains Emigrant Canyon, and continue for a total of 0.1 mile until you reach a **road (11)** on the west (right) side of the tracks. Look carefully for the road.

3.4 – 4.6   +450 **(11)** Leave the railroad tracks; ski south on the road described above for a short distance until you reach a road junction; turn north (right) onto and follow the road as it gradually turns west up Emigrant Canyon and crosses the creek in Emigrant Canyon for a total of 1.2 miles until you reach a location where the slope to the north becomes less steep **(12)**.

4.6 – 4.9 +150 **(12)** Turn north (right) and climb for 0.3 mile until you reach a **saddle (13)**.

4.9 – 5.2 –100 **(13)** Ski north for 0.3 mile until you reach the **railroad tracks (14)**. Be cautious of the steep drop as you approach the tracks. Eder, a fuel and water stop for locomotives, existed here once upon a time. Nearby you will see several of the snowsheds which protect portions of the Southern Pacific Railroad tracks.

5.2 – 6.4 –750 **(14)** Cross to the north side of the tracks; descend a short but very steep slope; descend gradually down Lakeview Canyon through the trees for 0.9 mile; finally descend at a steep angle through very dense woods for 0.3 mile until you reach the **plowed road (15)** near Donner Lake. There are also roads in Lakeview Canyon that you can descend if you encounter them.

You have completed this tour if your shuttle car is located here; otherwise you must return to the starting point.

6.4 – 8.1 –50 **(15)** Ski east along the shore of Donner Lake for 1.7 miles to **China Cove (2)**. As an alternative you can walk east on South Shore Drive for 1.3 miles until the road is no longer plowed and then ski east on the road for 0.4 mile to China Cove. In either case, at China Cove locate the marked ski trail that loops through Donner Memorial State Park.

8.1 – 8.6 +0 **(2)** Follow the marked trail (not the road along the lake) east for 0.5 mile until you reach a snow-covered **road (3)**.

8.6 – 9.0 +0 **(3)** Ski east on the road for 0.4 mile until you reach the location where the **road turns north (4)**.

9.0 – 9.2 +0 **(4)** Continue east (do not turn north with the marked ski trail) for 0.2 mile until you reach the first **road (6)** on which you skied.

9.2 – 9.6 +0 **(6)** Turn north (left) and ski on the road for 0.4 mile back to the **starting point (5)**.

MAP 10
PAGE 75

26 Schallenberger Ridge

Difficulty	4
Length	10 miles round trip
Elevation	5950/+1650,−1650
Navigation	Road and map
Time	Full day
Season	Late December through March
USGS topo	7.5' series, Truckee, Norden
Start	The entrance to the gravel pit just south of Interstate 80 where Donner Pass Road crosses it. This is located just south of two gas stations.

You can see the entire length of Schallenberger Ridge from north of Donner Lake on Interstate 80. Pick a clear day to ski along the ridge so that you can appreciate the locale and the outstanding scenery. To the north and directly below the ridge is Donner Lake. Farther north lie ridges which hide Euer and Carpenter valleys. To the southwest is the Mt. Lincoln-Anderson Peak ridge with its cornices and bowls. To the southeast is Coldstream Valley through which this tour passes.

Mileage Log

0.0 – 0.4   +0 **(5)** Ski south on the road for 0.4 mile until you reach a **road junction (6)**. This section may be plowed in times of low snow.

0.4 – 0.7   +100 **(6)** Ski on the east (left) fork until the road begins to climb, then climb at a steep angle for a total of 0.3 mile until you reach the location where the **road levels (7)**. At this location you leave the road, but you will return to this point at the end of the tour.

0.7 – 2.7   +1400 **(7)** Climb west up the steep east shoulder of Schallenberger Ridge and then along the ridge for a total of 2.0 miles until you reach the **summit of Peak 7469 (16)**. In this section you gain 1400 feet, almost all of the elevation gain for the loop, you cross a snow-covered road, and at one point, you can see where the railroad tracks below the ridge disappear into the mountainside.

The terrain along the ridge is a combination of wooded and open areas. When choosing your route, remember to stay back from the north edge of the ridge where it may be overhung.

2.7 – 3.4   +100,−200 **(16)** Descend and then ascend gradually west for 0.7 mile until you reach the next **peak (17)**.

3.4 – 3.9   +50,−150 **(17)** Descend southwest along a much narrower portion of the ridge for 0.5 mile until you reach **Peak 7264 (18)**, a high but not prominent point. Although there is adequate space on this ridge to ski, remember that the north edges may be overhung.

3.9 – 4.3 –400 **(18)** Descend southwest through trees for 0.4 mile until you reach a **saddle (13)** where you may be able to locate the road shown on the topo. To the north of the saddle is Eder, former site of a railroad stop. This tour heads south from the saddle although you can reach Donner Lake by skiing north following the Schallenberger Loop tour (no. 25).

4.3 – 4.6 –150 **(13)** Ski south, following the road if possible, for 0.3 mile into Emigrant Canyon until you reach the **creek (12)**.

4.6 – 5.8 –450 **(12)** Follow the road or creek east for a total of 1.2 miles until you reach the **railroad tracks (11)**. At the east end of Emigrant Canyon you must cross to the south side of the creek and then follow the road south to the railroad tracks.

5.8 – 9.2 –300 **(11)** Ski or walk north along the railroad tracks until you reach a location just northeast of the creek draining Emigrant Canyon; drop down to the southeast of the tracks; then ski northeast and parallel to them until you pickup the road heading northeast; finally follow the road northeast for a total of 3.4 miles until you reach the **starting point (5)**.

Railroad tracks in Coldstream Valley

27 Highway 89 North of Truckee

Difficulty	1 – 3
Length	At your discretion
Elevation	5800-6400/At your discretion
Navigation	Road and map
Time	Short to full day
Season	Late December through March
USGS topo	7.5' series, Truckee, Hobart Mills, Sierraville, Sardine Peak
Start	Highway 89 north of Truckee. From the Sierraville-Quincy exit on Interstate 80 or from Truckee, drive north on Highway 89 and park along the highway where you find an interesting place to ski. See the tour description for more information.

Drive north from Truckee on Highway 89 for 15 miles and you will be surprised at the abundance of fine touring terrain. This is an ideal place for spending a few hours or a whole day.

The area is made up of flat and rolling terrain and modest ridges. Prosser Creek, Sagehen Creek, and the Little Truckee River beckon you to ski along them. As a general rule, it is not difficult to find parking along the highway although in some places a shovel might be necessary to clear a place.

In addition to this tour, which leaves the choice of location up to you, the five tours (nos. 28-32) that follow describe specific tours in the same area.

A steep descent

MAP 11
PAGE 86

28 Sagehen Hills

Difficulty	4
Length	5 miles round trip
Elevation	6200/+900,–900
Navigation	Road, map and compass
Time	Half day
Season	January through mid-March
USGS topo	7.5' series, Hobart Mills
Start	Highway 89, 1.7 miles south of Sagehen Summit.

This tour to the summit of Sagehen Hills is short, but steep, which accounts for its rated difficulty. But it is the descent and the panoramic view from the summit that are the reason for visiting here.

Although this tour can be done completely on roads, the narrowness and steepness of the roads make that alternative a poor choice. Therefore, this tour descends the steepest terrain cross-country. The drawback is that this area, recovering from a major forest fire in the 1960s, is covered by small trees and manzanita. Thus, this tour is not recommended for early season skiing — make sure that there is adequate, well consolidated snow cover.

Mileage Log

The mileage log that follows assumes that you are starting where a side road intersects the west side of Highway 89. In the event that parking here is difficult, you should choose to park farther north. This will permit you to ski west from the highway, through trees, and intersect the route described.

0.0 – 0.1 +50 **(1)** Ski west on a road for 0.1 mile until you reach a **road junction (2)**.

0.1 – 0.2 +0 **(2)** Turn south (left) and ski on the road for 0.1 mile until you reach a **road junction (3)**. Look carefully for the small road on the west (right) side of the large road you are skiing on.

0.2 – 1.8 +600 **(3)** Take the west (right) fork and climb on it for 1.6 miles until you reach the **east ridge of Sagehen Hills (4)**.

1.8 – 2.1 +250 **(4)** Ascend west (left) up the ridge for 0.3 mile until you reach the **summit of Sagehen Hills (5)**. Be aware that the north side of the summit ridge may be corniced.

2.1 – 3.1 –700 **(5)** Ski north on the summit ridge to avoid the cornice and then descend slightly east of north, picking your best route for a total of 1.0 mile until you reach a **road (6)**. You will miss the intersection with the road shown on the map if you are too far east (right), but you will eventually intersect a road.

28

3.1 – 3.5   –150 **(6)** Descend north (right) on the road to the north for 0.4 mile until you reach a **road junction (7)**.

3.5 – 3.9   +0 **(7)** Turn southeast (right) onto the large road and ski 0.4 mile until you reach a **road junction (8)**.

3.9 – 4.4   +0 **(8)** Continue south (straight) on the large road for 0.5 mile until you reach the **road junction (2)** you were at previously.

4.4 – 4.5   –50 **(2)** Turn east (left) and ski 0.1 mile to the **starting point (1)**.

Exploring new route

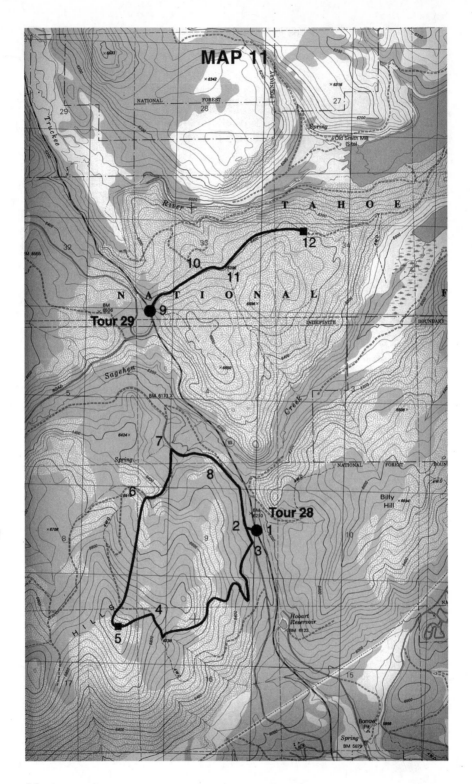

MAP 11
PAGE 86

Stampede Reservoir Overlook

29

Difficulty	2
Length	4 miles round trip
Elevation	6450/+50,−50
Navigation	Road
Time	Few hours
Season	Late December through mid-March
USGS topo	7.5′ series, Hobart Mills
Start	Sagehen Summit on Highway 89, 0.1 mile north of the University of California Sagehen Creek Field Station garage.

This short tour ends at an overlook above Stampede Reservoir where the landscape is stark. The near perfectly level route and an easy-to-follow road make this a perfect tour for beginners. Although not described here, more adventurous skiers can continue past the overlook on roads and descend to Stampede Reservoir. However, it will require climbing back out.

This entire area is covered with manzanita that took over after a fire in the 1960s. As a result, early in the season it is not possible to ski off the road.

Mileage Log

0.0 – 0.5   −50 **(9)** Ski northeast on the road for 0.5 mile until you reach a **road junction (10)**.

0.5 – 0.7   +0 **(10)** Take the east (right) fork and continue east for 0.2 mile until you reach a **road junction (11)**.

0.7 – 1.8   +0 **(11)** Take the north (left) fork and continue northeast for 1.1 miles until you reach the location where the **road begins to descend (12)** and there is a grand view of Stampede Reservoir below to the northeast.

Difficulty	1 to Kyburz Flat and 2 for Wheelers Sheep Camp Loop
Length	2 miles round trip to Kyburz Flat and 4 miles round trip for Wheelers Sheep Camp Loop
Elevation	6300/+50,–50 to Kyburz Flat and 6300/+50,–50 for Wheelers Sheep Camp Loop
Navigation	Road and marked trail to Kyburz Flat, and road, marked trail and map for Wheelers Sheep Camp Loop
Time	Few hours to half day
Season	Late December through mid-March
USGS topo	7.5' series, Sierraville, Sardine Peak
Start	Highway 89, 13.9 miles north of Interstate 80.

Kyburz Flat is a large, open area that is reached by way of an easy-to-follow road. Once there, you can make a short loop through the woods to Wheelers Sheep Camp and then return via the flats.

Located in the shadow of the Sierra Crest at 6300 feet elevation, this area does not receive a great deal of snow. However, average winter storms drop sufficient snow to permit skiing throughout the season. On the positive side, you will find this tranquil setting uncrowded.

Mileage Log

0.0 – 1.0 +50 **(1)** Ski east on the snow-covered road for 1.0 mile until you reach a **high point (2)**, in the trees, at the edge of Kyburz Flat.

Ski the short distance to Kyburz Flat and explore at your leisure or continue on the Wheelers Sheep Camp Loop as described below.

1.0 – 1.2 +0 **(2)** From the high point at the edge of Kyburz Flat, follow a road and marked trail northwest through the trees for 0.2 mile until you reach a **road junction (3)**.

1.2 – 1.6 +0 **(3)** Turn north (right) and follow the road and marked trail for 0.4 mile until you reach a **creek drainage (4)**. Near the drainage, on the right-hand side of the road, are the remains of Wheelers Sheep Camp.

1.6 – 1.9 +0 **(4)** Follow the road and marked trail for 0.3 mile until you reach a large ski tour marker and the **end of the marked trail (5)**.

1.9 – 2.5 +0 **(5)** Ski south into the Kyburz Flat; continue to ski south through the flat until you are adjacent to the high point you were at earlier; then ski into the trees for a total of 0.6 mile until you reach the **high point (2)**.

2.5 – 3.5   –50 **(2)** Ski west on the road for 1.0 mile until you reach the **starting point (1)**.

Rim encrusted tree

31 Kyburz Flat Big Loop

MAP 12
PAGE 92

Difficulty	2
Length	6 miles round trip
Elevation	6300/+250,–250
Navigation	Road, marked trail and map
Time	Half day
Season	Late December through mid-March
USGS topo	7.5′ series, Sierraville, Sardine Peak
Start	Highway 89, 13.9 miles north of Interstate 80.

This loop tour circles the north arm of Kyburz Flat, then crosses the flat to return. It is a larger version of the Kyburz Flat and Wheelers Sheep Camp Loop tour (no. 30). Both tours offer a tranquil, uncrowded setting.

Located in the shadow of the Sierra Crest at 3600 feet elevation, this area does not receive a great deal of snow. However, average winter storms drop sufficient snow to permit skiing throughout the season.

Mileage Log

0.0 – 1.0 +50 **(1)** Ski east on the snow-covered road for 1.0 mile until you reach a **high point (2)**, in the trees, at the edge of Kyburz Flat.

1.0 – 1.2 +0 **(2)** Follow a road and marked trail northwest through the trees for 0.2 mile until you reach a **road junction (3)**.

1.2 – 1.5 +150 **(3)** Turn northwest (left) and follow a road and a marked trail through the trees for 0.3 mile until you reach a **road junction (6)**.

1.5 – 3.6 +0 **(6)** Turn east (right) and follow the road and marked trail for 2.1 miles until you reach the **end of the road (7)**. Take the right fork at all road junctions in this section.

3.6 – 3.9 –150 **(7)** Follow the marked trail southeast until you reach the top of a clearing and then descend the clearing for a total of 0.3 mile until you reach the **edge of Kyburz Flat (8)**. Disregard the markers that turn east (left) part way down the clearing.

3.9 – 4.6 +50,–50 **(8)** Turn west (right) and ski across Kyburz Flat until you reach the **high point (2)**. This may well be the trickiest part of the tour — do not attempt it if this crossing sounds too difficult. Here is a hint: When you reach the edge of the flat after descending, sight along the edge of the flat, trees to the north (right), to locate an approximate destination on the far side of Kyburz Flat. Once on the far side you can scout around for the high point. Of course a compass will make this task easier.

31

4.6 – 5.6   –50 **(2)** Ski west on the road for 1.0 mile until you reach the **starting point (1)**.

Great day to be out with friends

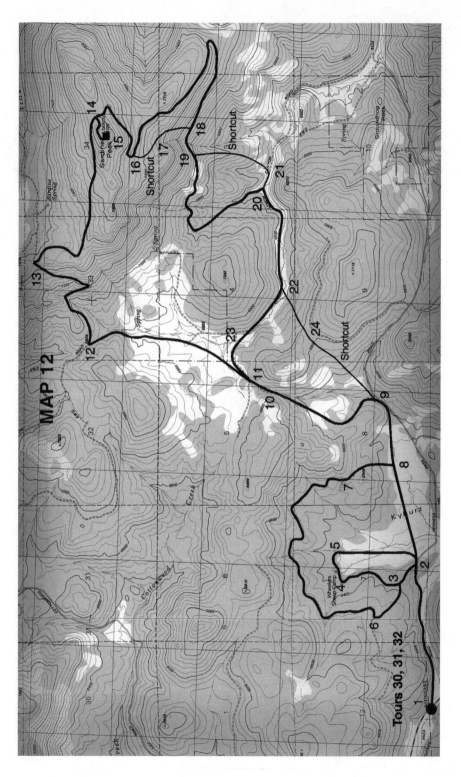

MAP 12

Tours 30, 31, 32

92

MAP 12
PAGE 92

Sardine Peak 32

Difficulty	4
Length	16 miles round trip (14 miles round trip with short cuts)
Elevation	6300/+2250,−2250
Navigation	Road, marked trail, map and compass
Time	Very long day
Season	Late December through mid-March
USGS topo	7.5′ series, Sierraville, Sardine Peak
Start	Highway 89, 13.9 miles north of Interstate 80.

Sardine Peak, with its panoramic views, offers an opportunity to kick-up-your-heels and cover a lot of miles over relatively easy terrain. In theory this tour is completely on roads, however, in reality the roads will not always be visible.

This tour's difficulty is primarily a consequence of the mileage. However, one shortcut includes a section of difficult skiing and another shortcut requires navigation with a compass.

Mileage Log

0.0 – 1.0   +50 **(1)** Ski east on the snow-covered road for 1.0 mile until you reach a **high point (2)**, in the trees, at the edge of Kyburz Flat.

1.0 – 2.2   +100,−50 **(2)** Ski east, across the flat, for 1.2 miles until you reach the **gap (9)** between Peak 6548 and Peak 7058.

2.2 – 3.1   +300 **(9)** Ski north for 0.9 mile until you reach second **gap (10)**.

3.1 – 3.3   +50 **(10)** Ski slightly east of north (right) for 0.2 mile until you reach a small, wooded **saddle (11)**. If in doubt, stay as far east (right) as possible while climbing gradually.

3.3 – 4.5   +200,−50 **(11)** Ski north across an open area, then up a road, for a total of 1.2 miles until you reach a **saddle and an obscure road junction (12)**.

4.5 – 5.6   +500 **(12)** Turn east (right) and zig-zag on the road for 1.1 miles until you reach a **saddle and road junction (13)**.

5.6 – 7.0   +600 **(13)** Turn south (right) and follow the road south and east for a total of 1.4 miles until you reach the east ridge of Sardine Peak and an obscure **road junction (14)**. The road that ascends to the summit will be obvious, but the road that crosses the ridge will not.

7.0 – 7.2   +150 **(14)** Turn west (right) and follow the road for 0.2 mile until you reach the **summit of Sardine Peak (15)**.

32

7.2 – 7.4 –150 **(15)** Retrace your tracks for 0.2 mile until you reach the **road junction (14)** on the east ridge of Sardine Peak.

7.4 – 8.0 –300 **(14)** Locate the road that descends from the ridge to the south (right) and follow it for 0.6 mile until you reach a **180-degree turn (16)** to the east (left). At this location the first shortcut leaves the road.

Continuing on the main route

8.0 – 11.0 –1200 **(16)** Continue to descend on the road for 3.0 miles until you reach **Lemon Canyon Road (20)**.

First shortcut

8.0 – 8.3 –300 **(16)** Leave the road at a 180-degree turn to the east (left) and descend southeast over moderate terrain for 0.3 mile until you reach the location where the **slope steepens abruptly (17)**. Make sure you are east (left) of the drainage that heads south.

8.3 – 8.5 –300 **(17)** Descend a very steep slope through more trees for 0.2 mile until you reach the **road (18).**

8.5 – 8.7 –100 **(18)** Ski west (right) on the road for 0.2 mile until you reach the **top of a spur (19)** that heads south.

8.7 – 9.3 –500 **(19)** Descend south on the spur for 0.6 mile until you reach **Lemon Canyon Road (21)**.

9.3 – 9.5 +0 **(21)** Turn west (right) onto the road and ski 0.2 mile until you reach a **road junction and the main route (20)**.

Continuing on the main route

11.0 – 11.8 +100 **(20)** Ski west on Lemon Canyon Road for 0.8 mile until you reach the location where it makes a **45-degree turn (22)** to the northwest (right). At this location the second shortcut leaves the road.

Continuing on the main route

11.8 – 12.3 +50 **(22)** Ski northwest on the road for 0.5 mile until you reach a **clearing (23)**.

12.3 – 12.6 +100 **(23)** Loop to the northwest and then southwest through the clearing, and then ascend for a total of 0.3 mile until you reach a **saddle (11)** on the route previously skied to Sardine Peak.

12.6 – 15.9 +50,–500 **(11)** Retrace your tracks for 3.3 miles to the **starting point (1)**.

Second shortcut

11.8 – 12.1 +300 **(22)** Leave Lemon Canyon Road at a 45-degree turn to the northwest (right) and ascend southwest (left) through dense but easily traversed woods to a **saddle (24)**.

12.1 – 12.8 –500 **(24)** Descend to the southwest, staying to the east (left) of the creek, for 0.7 mile until you reach the **gap (9)** between Peak 6548 and Peak 7058, and the route previously skied to Sardine Peak.

12.8 – 15.0 +50,–150 **(9)** Retrace your tracks for 2.2 miles until you reach the **starting point (1)**.

Take only pictures and leave only tracks

Backcountry solitude

North Tahoe

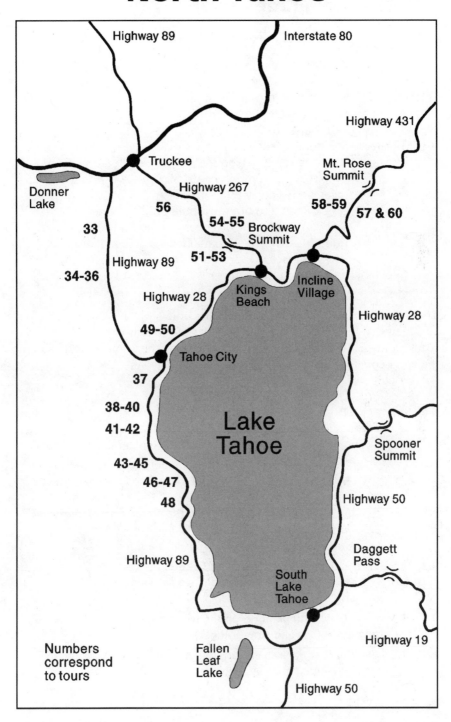

Highway 89

Interstate 80

Highway 431

Truckee

Mt. Rose
Summit

Donner
Lake

Highway 267

56

58-59

57 & 60

33

54-55 Brockway
Summit

51-53

Highway 89

34-36

Incline
Village

Highway 28

Kings
Beach

Highway 28

49-50

Tahoe City

37

38-40

Lake
Tahoe

41-42

Spooner
Summit

43-45

46-47

Highway 50

48

Daggett
Pass

Highway 89

South
Lake
Tahoe

Numbers
correspond
to tours

Fallen
Leaf
Lake

Highway 19

Highway 50

MAP 13
PAGE 100

33 Cabin Creek Loop

Difficulty	3
Length	4 miles round trip
Elevation	6250/+800,–800
Navigation	Road, marked trail and map
Time	Half day
Season	Late December through March
USGS topo	7.5′ series, Truckee
Start	Near the sanitary land fill which is located on Cabin Creek Road. From Interstate 80 drive south for 3.2 miles on Highway 89. Turn northwest onto Cabin Creek Road and drive 1.0 mile until the road levels and you reach a snow-covered road on the west (left) side of Cabin Creek Road. This point is marked with a Forest Service ski touring sign. You have gone too far if you reach the dump.

The Cabin Creek Loop is a short tour with a little bit of everything including fine views from breaks in the woods. Most of the tour is on snow-covered roads although there is one cross-country section. The whole route, including the cross-country section, was remarked in 1987 by volunteers.

Mileage Log

0.0 – 0.2 +100 **(1)** Ski west on the snow-covered road for 0.2 mile until you reach a **road junction (2)** where the loop begins and ends. You return to this point on the road from the south (left).

This tour is described in a counter-clockwise direction. However, you can change the descent on the narrow road paralleling the creek (miles 2.9-3.8) into an uphill climb by skiing this tour in the reverse direction. You may find this alternative preferable if you do not trust your control on a narrow road or when snow conditions are poor.

0.2 – 0.5 +0 **(2)** Turn north (right) and ski on the road for 0.3 mile until you reach a **fork in the road (3)**. The sanitary land fill is visible nearby to the east (right).

0.5 – 1.1 +0 **(3)** Continue north on the west (left) fork for 0.6 mile until you reach a **road junction (4)**.

1.1 – 1.2 +50 **(4)** Make a sharp turn to the west (left) and ski on the road for 0.1 mile until you reach another **road junction (5)**.

1.2 – 1.5   +200 **(5)** Turn onto the south (left) fork and ski 0.3 mile until until you reach a **sharp turn (6)** to the northwest (right).

1.5 – 2.1   +200 **(6)** Ski northwest on the road for 0.6 mile until you reach a **sweeping turn (7)** to the south (left). You can get good views toward Truckee by skiing off the road to the northeast just before you reach the turn.

2.1 – 2.3   +200 **(7)** Ski south on the road for 0.2 mile until you reach a **turn (8)** to the southwest. Up to this point, you have been climbing steadily, but just ahead the road crests and begins to descend.

2.3 – 2.7   –150 **(8)** Ski southwest on the road for 0.4 mile until you reach an **arrow (9)** on the south (left) side of the road indicating that the marked trail leaves the road. As you start to descend you can see Anderson Peak straight ahead.

> *The tour leaves the road at this point, however, an alternative is to continue down the road for 0.3 mile to its lowest point, then leave the road, and ski southeast down the drainage until you reach the narrow road described below.*

Site of airplane crash on Silver Peak

33

2.7 – 2.9 –150 **(9)** Leave the road on the marked trail and descend south into the drainage for 0.2 mile until you reach an old, narrow, rock-covered **roadbed (10)** which is marginal for skiing early and late in the season.

2.9 – 3.8 –400 **(10)** Descend the narrow road southeast along the creek for 0.9 mile until you reach a **larger road (11)**.

> *The manzanita bordering the narrow road can make skiing off the road difficult. One alternative is to cross to the southwest side of the creek and descend southeast along that side.*

3.8 – 4.1 +50 **(11)** Turn north (left) onto the larger road and ski 0.3 mile until you reach the first **road junction (2)**.

4.1 – 4.3 –100 **(2)** Turn east (right) and ski 0.2 mile back to the **starting point (1)**.

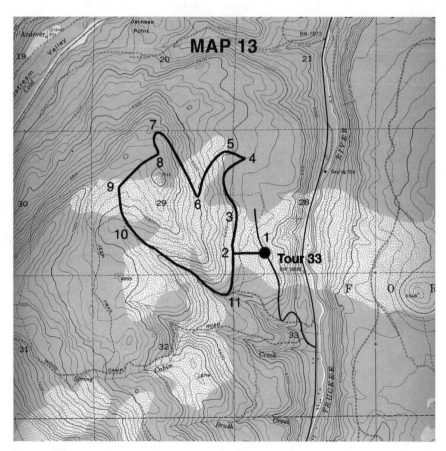

Slow going on steep climb

34 Pole Creek Loop

MAP 14
PAGE 103

Difficulty	3
Length	3 miles round trip
Elevation	6000/+650,−650
Navigation	Road
Time	Few hours
Season	Late December through mid-April
USGS topo	7.5′ series, Tahoe City
Start	West side of Highway 89, 6.5 miles south of Interstate 80, 8.0 miles north of Tahoe City, and immediately south of Pole Creek.

This short, easy-to-follow tour has considerable elevation gain. A little fresh snow helps give you confidence to enjoy the quick descent. Easy access, a road to follow, and protection from the wind make this tour ideal for bad weather conditions. Another good feature is that the area is closed to snowmobiles.

This tour is described as a clockwise loop. You can also ski the loop in the reverse direction, making the uphill steeper, but the downhill more gradual. Another alternative is to follow the route described to Pole Creek and return via the same route; although the distance is a little longer, the skiing is easier.

Mileage Log

0.0 – 1.7 +650 **(1)** Ascend the snow-covered road for 1.7 miles until you reach a **road junction (2)**. The west (left) fork heads to Silver Creek and is part of the Saddle Trail Loop and Silver Peak tours (nos. 35 and 36). This tour follows the north (right) fork.

1.7 – 2.2 −100 **(2)** Descend gradually on the north (right) fork for 0.5 mile, cross Pole Creek on a bridge, and encounter a **road junction (3)**.

> *Turn west (left) to lengthen the tour and follow the road, which climbs steadily and at a steep angle, for 2.6 mile until you reach a very distinct meadow. Along this section there are two road junctions. From the junction at the bridge, it is 0.9 mile to the first junction — stay left here. It is 1.6 miles farther to the second road junction — stay right here. The meadow is 0.1 mile ahead. Beware of avalanche conditions in the vicinity of the meadow.*

2.2 – 3.3 −550 **(3)** From the junction near the bridge follow the road east (right), paralleling the creek on its north side, for 1.1 miles until you reach **Highway 89 (4)**. This return route is a continuous downhill run, and the final 0.2 mile drops at a very steep angle. You may find it a good idea to walk the final 0.2 mile if snow conditions are poor. When you reach the highway you are 0.2 mile north of the starting point.

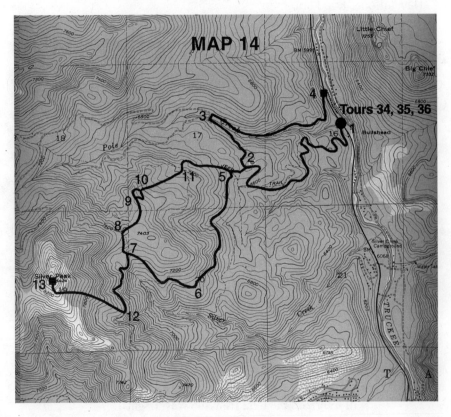

Difficulty	3
Length	7 miles round trip
Elevation	6000/+1400,−1400
Navigation	Road and map
Time	Half day
Season	Late December through mid-April
USGS topo	7.5' series, Tahoe City
Start	West side of Highway 89, 6.5 miles south of Interstate 80, 8.0 miles north of Tahoe City, and immediately south of Pole Creek.

This tour, originally marked by Big Chief Guides ski touring center (now defunct), combines touring on snow-covered roads with a short, wonderful ski along a broad ridge and a short descent through trees.

The Saddle Trail Loop tour begins by following the Pole Creek Loop tour (no. 34). Then it cuts off to make a 3-mile loop. Since it returns to the same location where it cut off, it can be used to lengthen the Pole Creek Loop tour. It can also be combined with the Silver Peak tour (no. 36).

Mileage Log

0.0 – 1.7 +650 **(1)** Ascend the snow-covered road for 1.7 miles until you reach a **road junction (2)**. The north (right) fork heads to Pole Creek and is part of the Pole Creek Loop tour. This tour follows the west (left) fork toward Silver Creek.

1.7– 1.8 +50 **(2)** Follow the west (left) fork and climb gradually for 0.1 mile until you reach a **road junction (5)**. You may miss this junction if it is not already tracked. At the end of this tour you will return on the road from the west (right).

1.8 – 2.8 +300 **(5)** Continue on the south (straight) fork, climbing gradually for 0.7 mile and then climbing at a steeper angle for 0.3 mile until you reach an obvious **overlook point (6)**. The excellent views from the overlook include Silver Peak to the west.

2.8 – 3.4 +300 **(6)** Continue on the road to the northwest for 0.6 mile until you reach an obscure **fork (7)** in the road. You will probably see a sign that says "Saddle Trail" with an arrow to the right. The obscure road to the south (left) is part of the Silver Peak tour.

3.4 – 3.6 +100 **(7)** Ski straight ahead (northwest) for a short distance and then veer north (right) for a total of 0.2 mile until you reach a broad **saddle (8)**. It is possible to descend the gully on the north side of the saddle to Pole Creek. However, the gully which is

35

broad and open at the top, narrows and is wooded near the bottom, and does not afford good skiing. Instead, this tour continues on the broad ridge to the northeast and north.

3.6 – 3.8 –100 **(8)** Ski northeast and then north along a broad ridge for 0.2 mile until you are **near the end of the ridge (9)**. On a large tree there is an arrow pointing east (right) and another arrow pointing toward the end of the ridge.

3.8 – 3.9 –100 **(9)** Descend 0.1 mile until you reach the **top of a clearing (10)** to the northeast. At the large tree described above you can either turn east (right) and loop around, or ski a short distance to the end of the ridge and then turn east (right) and loop around.

3.9 – 4.2 –250 **(10)** Ski northeast through the clearing for 0.3 mile until you reach a narrow **road (11)** that enters the trees. By staying on the south (right) side of the clearing as you approach the bottom you will funnel onto the road.

4.2 – 4.7 –250 **(11)** Ski north and then east on the road for a total of 0.5 mile until you reach a **road junction (5)**. The road you intersect is the road you followed to the saddle.

4.7 – 4.8 –50 **(5)** Turn east (left) and retrace your tracks for 0.1 mile until you reach a **road junction (2)**.

4.8 – 6.5 –650 **(2)** Turn east (right) and follow the road for 1.7 miles until you reach **Highway 89 (1)**.

Kicking steps on way to summit   by David Giese

36 Silver Peak

MAP 14
PAGE 103

Difficulty	4
Length	10 miles round trip
Elevation	6000/+2400,−2400
Navigation	Road and map
Time	Full day
Season	Late December through mid-April
USGS topo	7.5′ series, Tahoe City
Start	West side of Highway 89, 6.5 miles south of Interstate 80, 8.0 miles north of Tahoe City, and immediately south of Pole Creek.

From the small summit of Silver Peak, the views are magnificent in all directions. You can see Squaw Valley Ski Resort to the south, only 1.6 miles away but more than 2000 feet below. There are also excellent views of Lake Tahoe from both the ascent route and the summit.

The tour to the summit is for advanced skiers who seek either the summit of a windswept peak or excellent telemark terrain. If telemarking is your goal, pick a time when the snow is fresh or when spring conditions exist. Due to the elevation and orientation of the final ascent route, the snow near the summit tends to stay good for a considerable time after a new snowfall. However, much of this tour is through avalanche terrain and you must exercise appropriate care.

This tour to Silver Peak follows the Saddle Trail Loop tour (no. 35) for the first 3.4 miles. An interesting variation is to return via that loop.

Mileage Log

0.0 – 3.4   +1300 **(1)** Follow the Saddle Trail Loop tour (no. 35) for 3.4 miles until you reach an obscure **fork (7)** in the road. At the fork a sign says "Saddle Trail" with an arrow to the right. The tour to Silver Peak continues on the obscure road to the south (left).

3.4 – 3.9   +100 **(7)** Continue on the road to the south (left) for 0.5 mile until you reach the **entrance to a bowl (12)** that has a rock outcrop high above it on the ridge.

3.9 – 4.5   +1000 **(12)** Leave the road and ski northwest up a broad ridge; when the broad ridge disappears, continue to climb to the northwest and to the **summit of Silver Peak (13)**. For safety, stay in the sparse trees where possible. If the snow near the top is wind-packed, leave your skis near the last trees and hike the final 150 feet of elevation gain to the summit. In either case, as you approach the summit, head for a rock outcrop just to the south of the peak from where you can see the summit. To the south of the actual summit is a wooden cross and the remains of a crashed airplane.

Steep and fast   by Brenda Bowman

37 Truckee River

MAP 15
PAGE 109

Difficulty	2
Length	Up to 4 miles round trip
Elevation	6250/Nil
Navigation	Adjacent to road and map
Time	Few hours
Season	January through March
USGS topo	7.5′ series, Tahoe City
Start	Highway 89, anywhere between 0.1 and 0.3 mile south of the bridge across the Truckee River in Tahoe City.

The Truckee River provides a corridor along Highway 89 for cross-country skiers. When deep snow makes skiing difficult elsewhere or when you have only an hour or two to ski, this tour provides a pleasant opportunity to stretch your legs.

The background noise from the highway is a drawback to this tour. Also keep in mind that this tour requires crossing the Truckee River back and forth. Therefore, it can only be done when snow and temperature permits the crossing. Your exact route will depend on these conditions.

Mileage Log

0.0 – 0.4 +0 **(1)** Ski west for 0.4 mile until you reach a **drainage (2)** that heads south; power lines cross the river at this point. It may be necessary to take off your skis to cross a road in this section.

0.4 – 0.7 +0 **(2)** Ski west along the south side of the river, staying in the trees, for approximately 0.3 mile, and then descend to the **river (3)**. Descend to the river at a location where you can ski along it. In a heavy winter it may be possible to avoid this section in the trees.

0.7 – 1.2 +0 **(3)** Ski west along the river, crossing it where necessary, for 0.5 mile until you reach a **bridge (4)**.

Continue to ski west along the Truckee River until the conditions do not permit you to continue or until you choose to turn around.

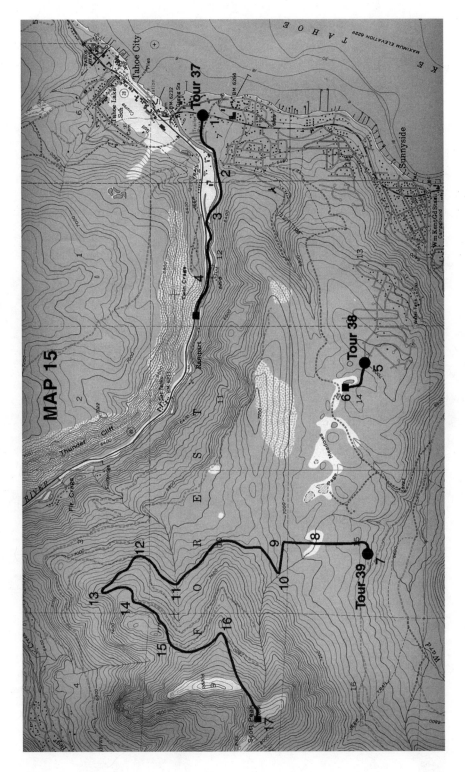

MAP 15

Following a backcountry track

MAP 15
PAGE 109

Paige Meadows **38**

Difficulty	2
Length	1 to 4 miles round trip
Elevation	7000/+100,–100
Navigation	Map
Time	Few hours to half day
Season	December through mid-April
USGS topo	7.5′ series, Tahoe City
Start	This tour begins in Talmont Estates. From the Tahoe City Bridge drive south on Highway 89 for 1.9 miles. Turn right onto Pine Avenue, after 0.2 mile turn right onto Tahoe Park Heights, after 0.7 mile turn right onto Big Pine Drive, and after 0.3 mile turn left onto Silver Tip Drive. Drive 0.5 mile until Club Drive goes to the left and Silver Tip Drive is no longer plowed. Park here.

Paige Meadows is not one meadow but a series of half-a-dozen interconnected meadows which have been protected from the sprawl of Lake Tahoe development. Beginners can appreciate the beauty of Sierra meadows in this scenic area. Because this area is slightly higher than the location of other beginner tours in the Lake Tahoe vicinity, you can enjoy more and better snow.

It is a short tour from the starting point to Paige Meadows. Once you ski into a meadow, the next one becomes visible. Since this pattern continues with each adjacent meadow, you can explore any number of them as you wish. For variation, ski in the woods which surround them.

Several notes are appropriate here: Most important, because of the multi-meadow configuration, take great care when entering Paige Meadows so that you can find your return route; it is easy to confuse the meadows and there are often many ski tracks. If you have been to Paige Meadows before and are thoroughly confident of your route-finding skills, Paige Meadows can be a pleasant location for a moonlight tour. Finally, when driving back to Highway 89, take a moment to admire Lake Tahoe from the intersection of Big Pine Drive and Tahoe Park Heights.

Mileage Log

0.0 – 0.2 +50,–50 (**5**) Ski in the direction Silver Tip Drive appears to continue until you reach a distinct crest; then descend straight ahead and down an open area until you enter the woods; continue on an obvious path that drops 50 feet quickly; and where the obvious route levels turn right and ski 50 yards through the trees until you reach the edge of **Paige Meadows (6)**.

Difficulty	3
Length	9 miles round trip
Elevation	6800/+1500,–1500
Navigation	Road, map and compass
Time	Full day
Season	December through mid-April
USGS topo	7.5′ series, Tahoe City
Start	From the bridge in Tahoe City, drive 2.5 miles south on Highway 89 to Pineland Drive. Turn right onto Pineland Drive and continue 0.4 mile until the road becomes Twin Peaks. Continue another 0.1 mile and the name of the road changes to Ward Creek Road. Drive 2.5 miles farther to Kitzbuhel Road (somewhere in this section Ward Creek Road will change name to Courcheval Road). Turn right onto Kitzbuhel and drive 0.2 mile to the dead end where the tour begins.

Although this tour is located in a wooded area near Tahoe City, it offers the peace and quiet of a more remote place. Along the route there are views of Paige Meadows and Lake Tahoe; the best ones are from the summit of Scott Peak where steep, corniced ridges to the north and west line the horizon. While it is not difficult to reach the summit, skiers who prefer a shorter tour can enjoy the rolling terrain near the starting point or a section of the tour.

This tour is predominantly on roads; only the very beginning and the final ascent require any navigation. The first 0.6 mile through woods without any landmarks poses the greatest difficulty.

Mileage Log

0.0 – 0.4 +150 **(7)** Ski east into the trees and almost immediately you reach a clearing. Turn and ski north, shortly after you turn you cross a road, and continue to ski north for a total of 0.4 mile until you reach the **largest of several small clearings (8)**.

0.4 – 0.6 +100 **(8)** Continue north (straight) through the woods for 0.2 mile until you reach a **road (9)** which is more obvious in some places than in others. The road you intersect heads east (right) to Paige Meadows.

0.6 – 0.8 +50 **(9)** Turn west (left) and ski on the road for 0.2 mile until you reach a **sharp turn (10)** to the northeast (right).

0.8 – 1.8 +100 **(10)** Ski generally north on the road for 1.0 mile until you reach a **creek (11)**.

1.8 – 2.2	+0 **(11)** Ski northeast on the road for 0.4 mile until you reach a **road junction (12)**.
2.2 – 2.5	+250 **(12)** Take the west (left) fork and ski northwest on the road for 0.3 mile until you reach a **turn (13)** to the south (left).
2.5 – 2.9	+50 **(13)** Ski south on the road for 0.4 mile until you reach a **road junction (14)**.
2.9 – 3.3	+100 **(14)** Take the west (right) fork and ski 0.4 mile until you reach another **road junction (15)** at a prominent saddle.
3.3 – 3.7	+200 **(15)** Take the west (right) fork and ski 0.4 mile until you reach an east-west **ridge (16)**.
3.7 – 4.4	+500 **(16)** Leave the road and climb steadily southwest for 0.5 mile until you reach the saddle between Scott Peak and Peak 8208, and then continue southwest for 0.2 mile until you reach the **summit of Scott Peak (17)**.

Lake Tahoe from Scott Peak

40   **Stanford Rock**

MAP 16
PAGE 115

Difficulty	3
Length	8 miles round trip from Ward Creek or 10 miles round trip from Highway 89
Elevation	6450/+2000,−2000 from Ward Creek or 6250/+2200,−2200 from Highway 89
Navigation	Road and map
Time	Full day
Season	Mid-December through mid-April
USGS topo	7.5' series, Tahoe City, Homewood
Start	From the bridge in Tahoe City, drive 2.5 miles south on Highway 89 to Pineland Drive. Turn right onto Pineland Drive and continue 0.4 mile until the road becomes Twin Peaks. Continue another 0.1 mile and the name of the road changes to Ward Creek Road. The starting point is exactly 0.9 mile ahead but do not expect to find parking here unless you bring a shovel. An alternate starting point is on Highway 89 on the south side of the bridge across Ward Creek, 0.4 mile south of Pineland Drive.

The tour to Stanford Rock offers spectacular views along the route as well as from the summit. When snow conditions are good, the continuous but moderate gradient offers a wonderful descent. However, if conditions are bad, this descent can be unpleasant due to icy spots on the narrow road. Plan this tour accordingly.

The standard Ward Creek route has only one major challenge — crossing Ward Creek at the start. Unfortunately, the tree that once spanned the creek is gone. You can either puddle jump at low water levels, or you can start on Highway 89 at the Ward Creek bridge.

Mileage Log

Beginning from Ward Creek

0.0 – 0.1   +50 **(1)** After crossing Ward Creek, ski south on the snow-covered road for 50 yards until you reach a road junction. The road to the east (left) zig-zags up to where the road to the south (straight) goes directly. Continue south for another 50 yards until you reach another **junction (2)** where the two roads meet along with the route from Highway 89.

Beginning from Highway 89

0.0 - 1.3 +250 **(3)** Ski west and parallel to Ward Creek for 1.2 miles until you intersect a road which seems to make a switchback; continue on the south (left) fork for 0.1 mile until you reach the **route from Ward Creek (2)** where a road crosses the one you are on. After leaving the highway, if you look carefully, there is an abandoned road creating a clear path. The clear route disappears about 0.4 mile from the start and you should veer slightly south until you intersect a well-defined roadbed.

Continuing on the combined
Ward Creek and Highway 89 routes with
mileages from the Ward Creek starting point

0.1 – 0.2 +100 **(2)** Ski southwest on the road for 0.1 mile until you reach a **turn (4)** to the east (left).

0.2 – 0.7 +150 **(4)** Ski east on the road for 0.5 mile until you reach a **road junction (5)**.The north (left) fork leads to the Timberland sub-division which, unfortunately, is not an acceptable starting point for the tour to Stanford Rock.

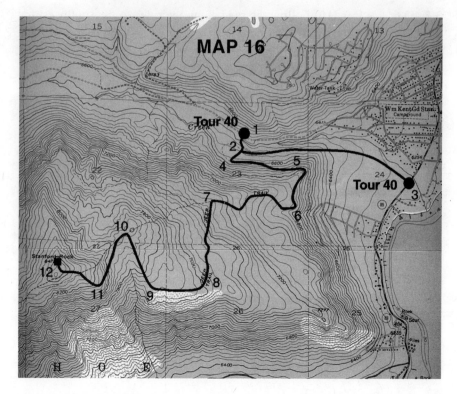

40

0.7 – 1.0 +100 **(5)** Ski on the south (right) fork for 100 yards until you you pass a very small road on your right; continue on the main road, which turns south (right), for 0.3 mile until you reach a **turn (6)** to the west (right).

1.0 – 1.7 +450 **(6)** Climb gradually west on the road for 0.7 mile until you reach a **turn (7)** to the south (left).

1.7 – 2.3 +300 **(7)** Ski south on the road for 0.3 mile until you reach a relatively flat and open area where you must look carefully for the road leaving the high side of the clearing; continue on the road for 0.3 mile until you reach a **ridge (8)**. In this last section between the clearing and the ridge, follow the road with care, especially when crossing an open area.

2.3 – 2.7 +100 **(8)** Cross the ridge and ski west on the road for 0.4 mile until you reach a **turn (9)** to the north (right). There is a spectacular view into Blackwood Canyon as you traverse above a steep slope before the road turns north.

2.7 – 3.2 +300 **(9)** Ski north on the road for 0.5 mile until you reach a **ridge (10)**.

3.2 – 3.6 +150 **(10)** Follow the road along the ridge to the southwest for 0.1 mile; then turn south and ski on the road for 0.3 mile until you reach a distinctive **view point (11)**.

3.6 – 4.0 +300 **(11)** Climb to the northwest for 0.4 mile until you reach the **summit of Stanford Rock (12)**. In this section, although you may not be able to discern the road, the route is obvious. At the summit, the striking view to the west is of Twin Peaks.

MAP 17
PAGE 118

Blackwood Canyon **41**

Difficulty	1
Length	Up to 6 miles round trip
Elevation	6200/+200,−200
Navigation	Road
Time	Up to half day
Season	Late December through early April
USGS topo	7.5' series, Homewood
Start	Kaspian Recreation Area on Highway 89, 4.4 miles south of the bridge in Tahoe City.

Wooded Blackwood Canyon is over four miles long. Stanford Rock, Twin Peaks, Barker Peak, and Ellis Peak are prominent on the ridges which flank the canyon and form the large bowl at its head. When planning your trip, keep in mind that this area is often used by snowmobilers.

Mileage Log

0.0 – 2.3 +200 **(1)** Ski west on the snow-covered road for 2.3 miles until you reach the **bridge (2)** that crosses Blackwood Creek. The road that crosses the bridge climbs steadily to Barker Pass and is described in the Barker Pass tour (no. 42).

2.3 – 3.2 +0 **(2)** Continue to ski southwest on the north side of the creek for 0.9 mile until you encounter **more difficult terrain (3)**.

Easy skiing along a Sierra creek   by Lyle Foster

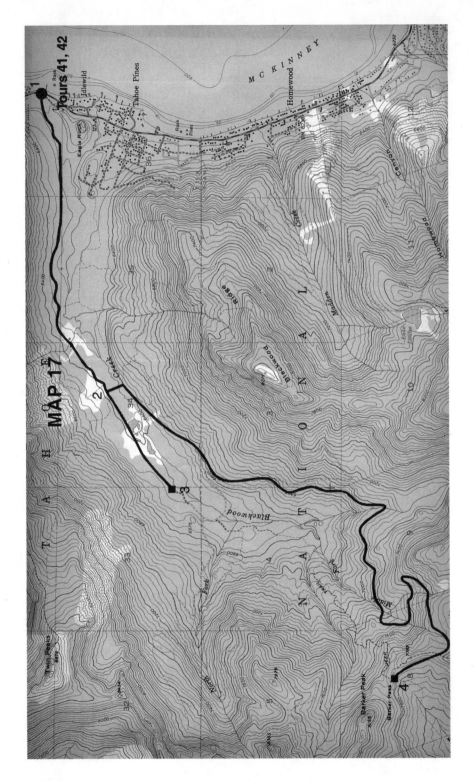

MAP 17
PAGE 118

Barker Pass 42

Difficulty	3
Length	14 miles round trip
Elevation	6200/+1450,−1450
Navigation	Road
Time	Full day
Season	Late December through early April
USGS topo	7.5′ series, Homewood
Start	Kaspian Recreation Area on Highway 89, 4.4 miles south of the bridge in Tahoe City.

Barker Pass offers a fine view of Blackwood Canyon to the northeast and a glimpse of Lake Tahoe. The beautiful canyon is surrounded by Stanford Rock, Twin Peaks, Barker Peak, and Ellis Peak. Barker Meadow is to the west of the pass and farther west is the Rubicon River.

Mileage Log

0.0 – 2.3 +200 **(1)** Ski west on the snow-covered road for 2.3 miles until you reach the **bridge (2)** that crosses Blackwood Creek. Up to this point you have been following the Blackwood Canyon tour (no. 41) which continues on the north side of Blackwood Creek.

2.3 – 7.1 +1250 **(2)** Cross the bridge to the south side of Blackwood Creek and climb at a steep angle on the road for 4.8 miles until you reach **Barker Pass (4)**.

43 Miller Meadows

Difficulty	2
Length	8 miles round trip
Elevation	6350/+750,–750
Navigation	Road
Time	Most of a day
Season	Late December through mid-April
USGS topo	7.5′ series, Homewood
Start	In McKinney Estates off Highway 89 about 8 miles south of Tahoe City. From Tahoe Ski Bowl Way which is at the southern boundary of Homewood, drive 1.2 miles south to McKinney Rubicon Springs Road. Turn west (right) onto McKinney Rubicon Springs Road and drive 0.3 mile where you turn left onto Bellevue Avenue. Continue for 0.2 mile where you turn right onto McKinney Road (Springs Court) and in another 0.3 mile turn left onto McKinney Rubicon Springs Road once again. In 0.1 mile you intersect Evergreen Way. This intersection is where the tour begins.

You have overcome the only navigational challenge if you have reached the starting point of the tour. Now you can enjoy a pleasant tour through a very scenic area.

You can extend the tour to Miller Meadows by skiing another mile to Richardson Lake and the Sierra Club's Ludlow Hut. That route is described in the Richardson Lake tour (no. 44).

Mileage Log

0.0 – 1.5   +300 **(1)** Ski on the snow-covered continuation of McKinney Rubicon Springs Road for 1.5 miles until you reach the bridge at **McKinney Creek (2)**.

1.5 – 2.4   +250 **(2)** Ski west on the road for 0.9 mile until you reach a location above and to the north of **McKinney Lake (3)**.

2.4 – 3.3   +200 **(3)** Ski west on the road for 0.9 mile until you reach **Lily Lake (4)**.

3.3 – 3.9   +0 **(4)** Ski west on the road for 0.6 mile until you reach **Miller Lake (5)**. In the past, the cabin marked on the topo at the north edge of Miller Lake made a nice shelter for lunch during cold, windy weather; regretfully it no longer exists.

3.9 – 4.2   +0 (5) Ski west on the road for 0.3 mile until you reach **Miller Meadows (6)**.

> *The section from Lily Lake to Miller Meadows is flat, and you can ski across Lily and Miller lakes if they are well-frozen.*

Road makes navigation easy

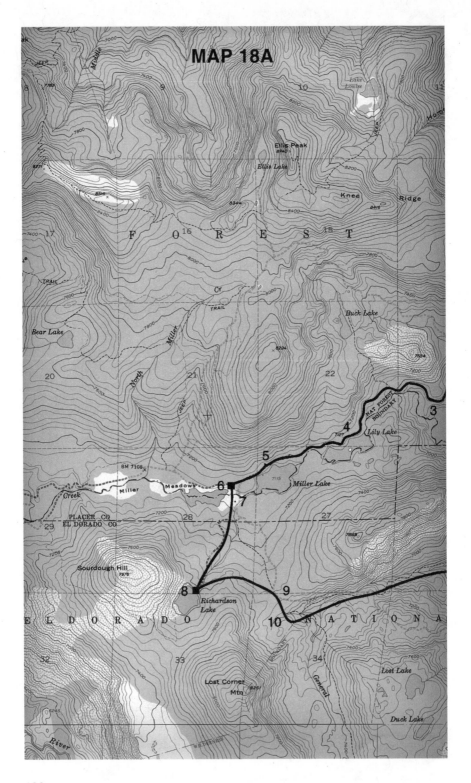

MAP 18A

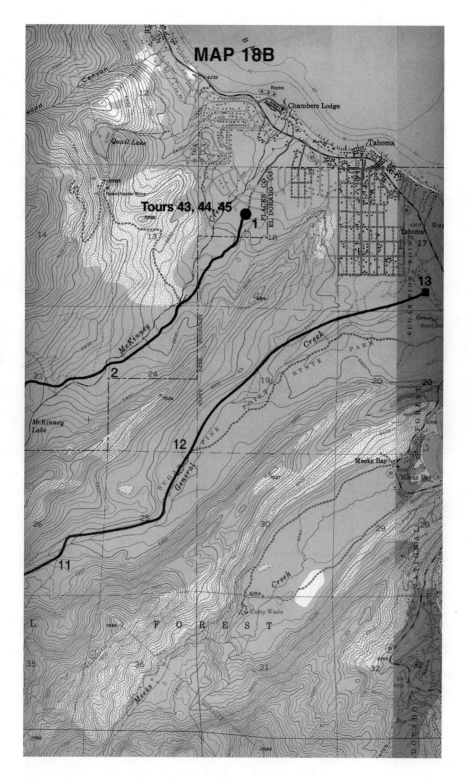

MAP 18B

Tours 43, 44, 45

44 Richardson Lake

Difficulty	3
Length	10 miles round trip
Elevation	6350/+1050,−1050
Navigation	Road and map
Time	Full day
Season	Late December through mid-April
USGS topo	7.5′ series, Homewood
Start	In McKinney Estates off Highway 89 about 8 miles south of Tahoe City. Detailed directions are given in the Miller Meadows tour (no. 43).

Richardson Lake is a beautiful spot to relax and eat a leisurely lunch. Although Richardson Lake is only a short distance from Miller Meadows, the extra mile increases the difficulty level because it requires navigation through dense woods.

Ludlow Hut, built by the Sierra Club in 1955, is located at Richardson Lake. For reservations contact:

> Clair Tappaan Lodge
> P.O. Box 36
> Norden, California 95724
> (916) 426-3632

Most skiers will choose to retrace their tracks after reaching Richardson Lake. If you are more adventuresome, you can return to Highway 89 via General Creek. Refer to the McKinney Creek and General Creek Loop tour (no. 45) for details.

Mileage Log

0.0 – 4.2   +750 **(1)** Follow the Miller Meadows tour (no. 43) for 4.2 miles until you reach **Miller Meadows (6)**.

> *Between Miller Lake and Miller Meadows, there is a road that heads south from the road you are on. You can reach Richardson Lake by following that road south for 0.9 mile; unfortunately it is a difficult road to spot or follow. The following is an alternative to that road.*

4.2 – 4.3   +0 **(6)** From the east end of Miller Meadows ski south for 0.1 mile until you reach several old **structures (7)**.

4.3 – 5.0   +300 **(7)** Follow the creek that drains Richardson Lake south for 0.7 mile until you reach the **lake (8)**. You can also follow a compass bearing to the lake. Ludlow hut is located about 100 yards east of the lake and slightly above it; about where the "L" is in "Richardson Lake" on the 1955 topo.

Tranquil Sierra meadow

45 McKinney Creek and General Creek Loop

MAP 18A-18B
PAGE 122-123

Difficulty	4
Length	11 miles one-way
Elevation	6350/+1050,−1100
Navigation	Road, marked trail, map and compass
Time	Full day
Season	January through March
USGS topo	7.5' series, Homewood, Meeks Bay
Start	In McKinney Estates off Highway 89 about 8 miles south of Tahoe City. Detailed directions are given in the Miller Meadows tour (no. 43).
End	Ski touring trailhead in Sugar Pine Point State Park on Highway 89, 0.8 mile south of Tahoma.

This challenging tour covers the wide variety of terrain of both the Richardson Lake tour (no. 44) and General Creek tour (no. 47), and a more difficult section in the upper reaches of General Creek where you can expect slow going. You will feel a sense of accomplishment upon the completion of this tour.

Since the entire south side of the ridge dominated by Peak 7859 is subject to avalanches, ski this tour only when the snow is stable.

Mileage Log

0.0 – 5.0 +1050 **(1)** Follow the Richardson Lake tour (no. 44) for 5.0 miles until you reach **Richardson Lake (8)**.

5.0 – 5.6 −50 **(8)** Traverse through the trees and around the north ridge of Lost Corner Mountain for 0.6 mile until you reach the very broad **saddle (9)** between Lost Corner Mountain and Peak 7859. A good reference point, Peak 7859, is occasionally visible as you traverse.

5.6 – 5.7 −100 **(9)** Descend along the route of the summer trail for 0.1 mile until you reach **General Creek (10)**. Cross to its south side in order to avoid a rock buttress of Peak 7859.

5.7 – 7.4 −650 **(10)** Descend east along General creek for 1.7 miles until you reach the **creek draining Duck Lake (11)**. The skiing in this section is very difficult and you can expect to spend one to two hours climbing over, around, up, and down boulders, trees, and cliffs. At the creek from Duck Lake you may want to cross back to the north side of General Creek.

7.4 – 8.8 −100 **(11)** Ski east along General Creek for 1.4 miles as the terrain rapidly opens up and the skiing becomes easier and more pleasurable until you reach the General Creek **marked ski touring trail (12)**. You should intersect the ski touring trail near where it crosses General Creek.

8.8 – 10.9   –200 **(12)** Follow the ski touring trail for 2.1 miles until you reach the **ending point (13)** at Sugar Pine Point State Park.

Helicopter skiing!

46 Sugar Pine Point State Park

MAP 19
PAGE 129

Difficulty	1
Length	Up to 2 miles round trip
Elevation	6300/Nil
Navigation	Marked trail
Time	Few hours
Season	Late December through March
USGS topo	7.5' series, Meeks Bay, Homewood; trail map available at trailhead
Start	Ski touring trailhead in Sugar Pine Point State Park on Highway 89, 0.8 mile south of Tahoma.

There are two very easy trails for beginners in Sugar Pine Point State Park; one is a loop in the campground area and the other is a loop on the east side of Highway 89 along the shore of Lake Tahoe. Both of these marked trails begin at the ski touring trailhead along with a longer, third tour which is also suitable for beginners. This longer tour is described in the General Creek tour (no. 47).

Sugar Pine Point State Park is open all winter for camping. Hot water and heated restrooms are provided in the campground which is quite during the winter months.

Note the form!

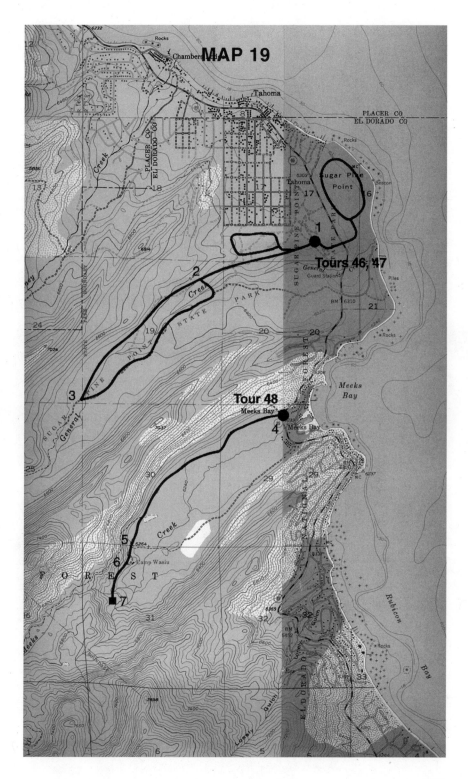

MAP 19

Tours 46, 47

Tour 48

129

47 General Creek

MAP 19
PAGE 129

Difficulty	2
Length	4 miles round trip
Elevation	6300/+150,−150
Navigation	Marked trail
Time	Half day
Season	Late December through March
USGS topo	7.5′ series, Meeks Bay, Homewood; trail map available at trailhead
Start	Ski touring trailhead in Sugar Pine Point State Park on Highway 89, 0.8 mile south of Tahoma.

Away from the annoying highway and snowmobiles, this area is a very pleasant place to ski. Beginners planning to ski here should also read the Sugar Pine Point State Park tour (no. 46) description.

Mileage Log

0.0 – 0.9   +0 **(1)** Follow the marked trail for 0.9 mile until you reach a **trail junction (2)**.

0.9 – 2.1   +150 **(2)** Ski southwest along the north side of General Creek for 1.2 miles until you reach the location where the **marked trail crosses to the south side of the creek (3)**.

2.1 – 3.4   −150 **(3)** Ski northeast along the south side of General Creek for 1.3 miles until you reach the location where the **marked trail crosses to the north side of the creek (2)**.

3.4 – 4.3   +0 **(2)** Retrace your tracks for 0.9 mile until you reach the **starting point (1)**.

MAP 19
PAGE 129

Meeks Creek 48

Difficulty	1 – 2
Length	Up to 4 miles round trip
Elevation	6200/Up to +200,–200
Navigation	Road
Time	Few hours
Season	Late December through March
USGS topo	7.5' series, Meeks Bay, Homewood
Start	Meeks Bay on Highway 89 about 12 miles south of Tahoe City and 17 miles north of the intersection of Highways 50 and 89 in South Lake Tahoe.

Meeks Creek is located in a heavily wooded valley through which you travel on a level and easy-to-follow road. This protected area is an excellent location to ski during a storm.

The tour begins at the building on the west side of the highway and on the north side of Meeks Creek, and follows the adjacent road. This road is also the beginning of the well-known Tahoe to Yosemite Trail.

Mileage Log

0.0 – 1.5   +100 **(4)** Ski southwest on the road for 1.5 miles until you reach the **location where it starts to climb (5)**.

1.5 – 1.7   +50 **(5)** Ski on the road for 0.2 mile until you reach an **abandoned cabin (6)**.

1.7 – 2.0   +50 **(6)** Ski on the road for 0.3 mile until you reach the **end of the valley (7)**.

49 Painted Rock Loop

Difficulty	3
Length	9 miles round trip
Elevation	6600/+1100,–1100
Navigation	Road, marked trail and map
Time	Full day
Season	Mid-December through early April
USGS topo	7.5′ series, Kings Beach, Tahoe City
Start	North Tahoe High School. From the main intersection in Tahoe City, drive 2.8 miles northeast on North Lake Blvd. (Highway 28) to the Dollar Hill Shell Station. At the gas station turn left onto Fabian Way, drive for 0.1 mile and turn right onto Village Road. Drive another 0.2 mile and turn left onto Polaris Road and follow it for 0.7 mile to North Tahoe High School.

You should plan this tour for a clear day so you can enjoy the view of Lake Tahoe and the wide variety of ski touring terrain. This tour takes you on marked (groomed) trails, snow-covered roads, and steep slopes.

As you read the following description of the route, note that there are many road junctions. Take sufficient time to follow the description carefully in order to save a great deal of time in the end.

On this tour, you travel on Burton Creek State Park roads which have been groomed by Tahoe Nordic Ski Center. Ordinarily, you are expected to pay for skiing on them. However, according to the District Superintendent of the Department of Parks and Recreation, you can ski on them without paying a fee as long as the trails are on public lands. Since this condition will prevail as long as skiers do not abuse the privilege, please abide by the following rules: do not ski on trails located on private property (all trails described in this tour are located in the public park or in the national forest); ski off the track if you are headed in the direction opposite to the groomed trail traffic.

Up to and including the winter of 1985, Tahoe Nordic marked road junctions with letters. The letters which were used in the winter of 1985 are indicated in parentheses, but realize that Tahoe Nordic may change them at any time.

Mileage Log

0.0 – 0.2   +0 **(1)** Ski west on the unplowed extension of Polaris Road for 0.2 mile until you reach a **road junction (2)**. Shortly after starting, you pass the "Burton Creek State Park" sign marking the entrance.

0.2 – 0.5 –100 **(2)** Turn south (left) and ski on the road for 0.3 mile until you reach at **turn (3)** to the northwest. Near this point, you may see another road heading northeast or another one heading south.

0.5 – 0.8 +50 **(3)** Ski northwest on the road for 0.3 mile until you are near **Burton Creek (4)**.

0.8 – 1.1 +50 **(4)** Ski on the road along the north side of the creek for 0.3 mile until you reach a **road junction (M) (5)**. In the winter of 1985, the groomed tracks continued along the road to the north (right). On this tour, you want the road to the northwest (left) which parallels the creek.

1.1 – 1.6 +100 **(5)** Ski northwest (left) on the road and along the creek for 0.3 mile until you cross a small creek and then for 0.2 mile until you reach a **road junction (I) (6)**.

1.6 – 1.6 +0 **(6)** Continue on the road that heads north (right) until you reach another **road junction (F) (7)** shortly thereafter.

1.6 – 2.5 +150 **(7)** Ski on the road to the northwest (left) and parallel to Burton Creek, which is out of sight, for 0.9 mile until you reach another **road junction (G) (8)**.

2.5 – 2.7 +100 **(8)** Leave the creek and follow the road to the north (right) for 0.2 mile until you reach yet another **road junction (H) (9)**.

2.7 – 3.0 +100 **(9)** Climb gradually on the road that heads west (left) for 0.3 mile until you reach a level section of road where, with careful observation, you can find an **abandoned road (10)** heading north (right) from the road you are on. Note that in the winter of 1994 the abandoned road appeared considerably more overgrown than in 1985. However, 1994 was plagued with very poor snowfall.

> *From this junction, you now ski a loop which starts on the road to the north (right) and returns on the road to the west (straight).*

3.0 – 3.4 +150 **(10)** Climb steadily north (right) on the abandoned road for 0.4 mile until you reach a **gully (11)** and the road vanishes.

3.4 – 3.7 +350 **(11)** Climb northwest at a very steep angle and through trees until you reach the saddle located on the ridge just north of Peak 7643; then continue north (right)for a total of 0.3 mile until you reach a well defined **road (12)**. This is an excellent location to have lunch; you can enjoy the views of Lake Tahoe, Mt. Watson, Peak 7908, and Painted Rock.

3.7 – 3.8   +50 **(12)** Ski north (left) on the road for 0.1 mile until you reach a **fork (13)**. The road to the northwest (right) leads to Starratt Pass; you want the road to the west (left).

3.8 – 4.5   –200 **(13)** Gradually descend west (left) on the road for 0.7 mile, as it traverses below Peak 7908, until you reach a **road junction (14)** where the road levels and turns south. From here it is a steep 350-foot climb to the top of Painted Rock. Avoid the northern slopes of Painted Rock which are prone to avalanche.

4.5 – 5.4   –300 **(14)** Descend on the road to the south, which follows a drainage, for 0.9 mile until you reach a **road junction (15)**. Do not take the road which climbs to the south.

5.4 – 5.9   –50 **(15)** Turn northeast (left) and follow the road as it weaves east for 0.5 mile until you reach the **junction (10)** with the abandoned road.

5.9 – 8.9   –450 **(10)** Retrace your tracks to the **starting point (1)**. Remember to ski off the groomed tracks because you will be skiing in the opposite direction of traffic.

Enjoying the views   by Lee Griffith

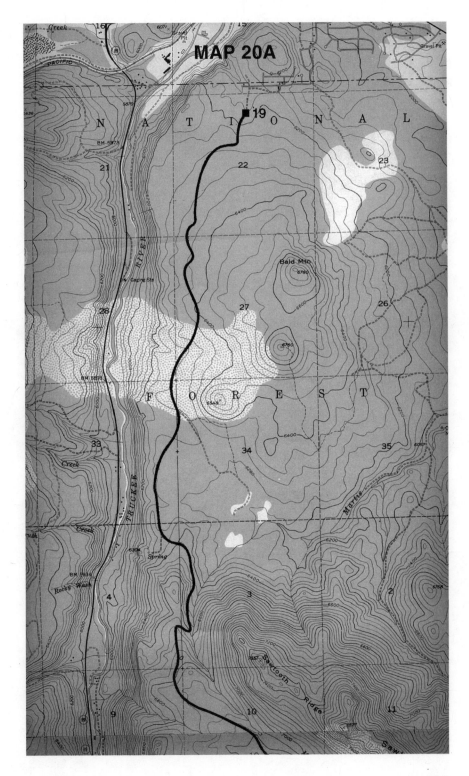

MAP 20A

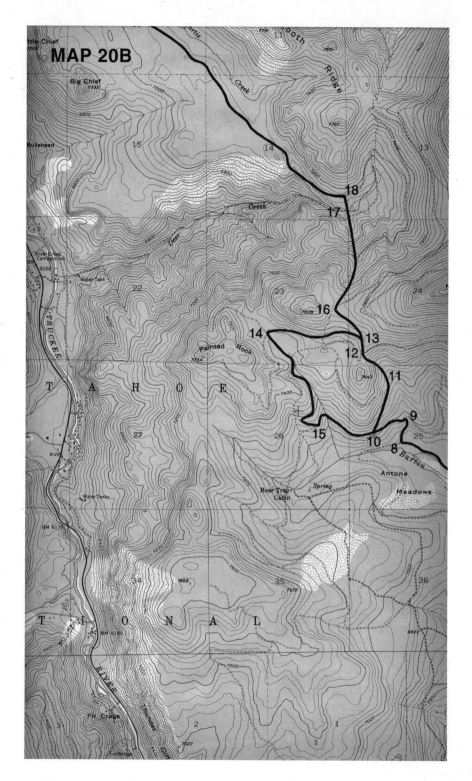

MAP 20B

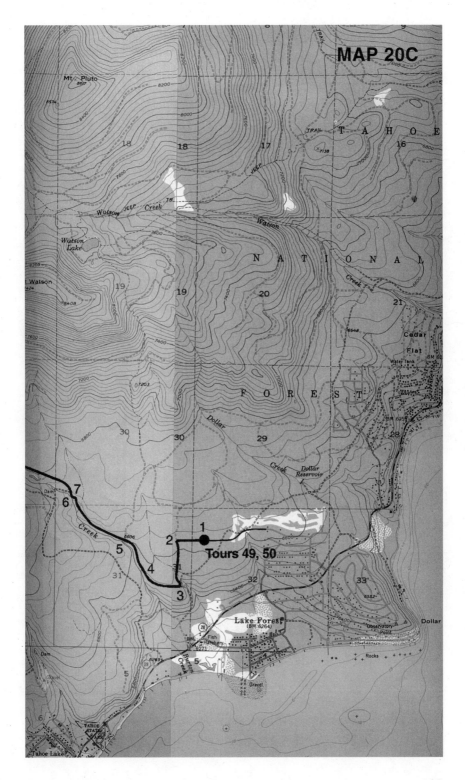

MAP 20C

Mt. Pluto

Watson Lake

Watson

Tours 49, 50

Lake Forest

Tahoe State Park

Tahoe Lake

Dollar Reservoir

Cedar Flat

Dollar

NATIONAL FOREST

TAHOE

50

Tahoe City to Truckee

Difficulty	4
Length	14 miles one-way
Elevation	6600/+1400,–1800
Navigation	Road, marked trail, map and compass
Time	Full day
Season	Late December through March
USGS topo	7.5' series, Kings Beach, Tahoe City, Truckee
Start	North Tahoe High School. From the main intersection in Tahoe City, drive 2.8 miles northeast on North Lake Blvd. (Highway 28) to the Dollar Hill Shell Station. At the gas station turn left onto Fabian Way, drive for 0.1 mile and turn right onto Village Road. Drive another 0.2 mile and turn left onto Polaris Road and follow it for 0.7 mile to North Tahoe High School.
End	Ponderosa Palisades subdivision in Truckee. From the main intersection in downtown Truckee drive southeast for 0.5 mile on Highway 267 and turn right onto Palisades Road. Continue for 0.3 mile until the road curves right and in another 0.1 mile you are forced to make a left turn onto Ponderosa Drive. Drive for 0.5 mile and turn right onto Silver Fir Drive. Drive for 0.4 mile and turn left onto Thelin Drive. A gate on the right side of the road, 0.2 mile ahead, marks the ending point.

This tour covers much of the same terrain as the The Great Ski Race which is sponsored each year by Tahoe Nordic Ski Center. With the aid of a groomed track, racers have completed the distance in less than two hours. Without the groomed track, you may find the slower pace more desirable since it affords you countless opportunities to appreciate the spectacular views of Lake Tahoe, the high peaks to the west of the Truckee River, and the mountains to the north.

Mileage Log

0.0 – 3.0   +550,–100 **(1)** Follow the Painted Rock Loop tour (no. 49) for 3.0 miles until you reach the **junction (10)** with the abandoned road. Tour 49 also provides information about skiing on the groomed trails in this area.

You can shorten this tour by following the Painted Rock Loop tour for another 0.8 miles to a fork (13) to the south

50

of Starratt Pass. That tour continues north from the junction (10) on the abandoned road. The tour described here continues on the main road and The Great Ski Race route.

3.0 – 3.5 +50 **(10)** Ski west on the main road for 0.4 mile until you cross a creek drainage and then for another 0.1 mile until you reach a **road junction (15).**

3.5 – 4.4 +300 **(15)** Continue on the north (right) fork, climb west, and then climb north for a total of 0.9 mile until the road levels and you reach a **road junction (14)** at a turn.

4.4 – 5.1 +200 **(14)** Continue on the east (right) road, which traverses below Peak 7908, for 0.7 mile to a **road junction (13).**

5.1 – 5.4 +100 **(13)** Turn northwest (left) and ski on the road for 0.3 mile until you reach **Starratt Pass (16).**

5.4 – 6.1 –650 **(16)** Leave the road which continues northeast and descend to the north along the steep drainage for 0.7 mile until you reach **Deer Creek (17).** In the drainage which you descend and elsewhere along this tour you may see markers denoting the Truckee Sierra Skiway. It is believed that these markers first appeared in the 1960s as part of an industrious effort to mark a ski trail system in the Sierra.

6.0 – 6.1 +50 **(17)** Climb north for 0.1 mile until you reach a **road (18).**

6.1 – 13.5 +150,–1050 **(18)** Turn northwest (left) onto the road and ski 7.4 miles until you reach the **ending point (19).** Because the road descends gradually or is level for most of the distance, you must pay close attention so you do not lose it. Use landmarks, such as Sawtooth Ridge, Martis Creek, Bald Mountain, and subtle changes in terrain to help you establish your location. You may also encounter some markers along the way but do not plan to rely on them.

51 Brockway Summit to Agate Bay

Difficulty	3
Length	2 miles one-way
Elevation	7200/–750
Navigation	Road
Time	Short
Season	Late December through March
USGS topo	7.5′ series, Martis Peak, Kings Beach
Start	Just south of Brockway Summit on Highway 267. Park in the plowed area on the west side of the highway.
End	A housing development adjacent to Agate Bay. From North Lake Blvd. (Highway 28), drive northwest on Agate Road for 0.4 mile to Tripoli Road. Turn right and drive 0.1 mile to the first road on your left. This is Old Wood Road or USFS Road 16N02. If you reach Granite Road you have gone too far. Even if it is possible to drive up Old Wood Road, it is best to park near its junction with Tripoli Road.

The entirely downhill run and the good views of Lake Tahoe are the highlights of this tour. Ski this short but steep tour if you want to liberate that final bit of energy which remains after completing one of the other tours in the Brockway Summit area. Better yet, if you are fortunate to wake up early to a fresh snowfall, leave behind those who chose to party the night before and enjoy the descent before the route is tracked. When you return to the cabin you can gloat in the exhilaration of your early morning descent as you consume an extra portion of well deserved blueberry pancakes.

In the past, this route along USFS roads took skiers from the starting point to Carnelian Bay. Unfortunately, due to construction, the tour now terminates in the Agate Bay housing development. Another disappointing change is that the Forest Service has granted a permit to rent snowmobiles at the starting point of this tour. Where once there was moderate snowmobile use on weekends, there is now heavy use on weekends and moderate use mid-week.

Mileage Log

Very close to the starting point is a radio tower and small building. You begin the tour by skiing southwest on Mt. Watson Road which is visible near the tower. Do not confuse this road with another that descends to the south.

0.0 – 0.3   +0 (1) Ski southwest on level Mt. Watson Road for 0.3 mile until you reach a **road junction (2)**. The north (right) fork leads to Sawmill Flat and is part of the Brockway Summit to Tahoe

City and Brockway Summit to Northstar tours (nos. 52 and 53). You want the south (left) fork which is Old Wood Road.

0.3 – 1.0 –250 **(2)** Descend on the south (left) fork, Old Wood Road, for 0.7 mile until you reach snow-covered **Regency Street (3)**.

1.0 – 1.2 –200 **(3)** Descend south (straight) on the road for 0.2 mile until you reach a sharp left **turn (4)**.

1.2 – 1.9 –300 **(4)** Continue on the road for 0.6 mile until you reach a housing development where the road is plowed; then either ski parallel to or walk on the road for 0.1 mile to the **ending point (5)** on Tripoli Road.

Perfect spring touring

52 Brockway Summit to Tahoe City

MAP 21A-21B
PAGE 144-145

Difficulty	3
Length	5 miles one-way
Elevation	7200/+250,–750
Navigation	Road
Time	Half day
Season	Late December through March
USGS topo	7.5′ series, Martis Peak, Kings Beach
Start	Just south of Brockway Summit on Highway 267. Park in the plowed area on the west side of the highway.
End	West end of Fulton Crescent in Cedar Flat. From the main intersection in Tahoe City, drive northeast on North Lake Blvd. (Highway 28) for 3.5 miles to Old County Road. Turn north onto Old County Road, drive for 0.7 mile, and turn right onto La Crosse Drive. At the tee intersection 0.3 mile ahead, turn left onto Fulton Crescent and drive 0.1 mile to its end.

Like the Brockway Summit to Agate Bay tour (no. 51), this downhill run to Tahoe City offers excellent views of Lake Tahoe. Unlike the short tour to Agate Bay, this longer tour to Tahoe City seems to justify the extra effort of running a car shuttle.

Those who have enjoyed touring in this area in years gone by will be disappointed in that the Forest Service has granted a permit to rent snowmobiles at the starting point of this tour. Where once there was moderate snowmobile use on weekends, there is now heavy use on weekends and moderate use mid-week.

Mileage Log

Very close to the starting point is a radio tower and small building. You begin the tour by skiing southwest on Mt. Watson Road which is visible near the tower. Do not confuse this road with another that descends to the south.

0.0 – 0.3   +0 **(1)** Ski southwest on level Mt. Watson Road for 0.3 mile until you reach a **road junction (2)**.

0.3 – 0.9   +150 **(2)** Ski on the north (right) fork for 0.6 mile until you reach a **road junction (6)** with a lesser road to the east (left).

0.9 – 1.2   +100 **(6)** Ski straight on Mt. Watson Road for 0.3 mile until you reach an obvious **vista point (7)** where the view of Lake Tahoe is superb.

1.2 – 2.6   –350 **(7)** Ski west on Mt. Watson Road for 1.4 miles until you reach **Sawmill Flat (8)**. When you encounter road junctions along this section, always follow Mt. Watson Road, the main road which heads west and downhill. When Mt. Watson Road becomes level, several roads intersect and head south. The first one is USFS Road 16N48, 0.1 mile farther west is another, and still 0.1 mile farther west is a major junction at Sawmill Flat.

At Sawmill Flat, the road to the north heads downhill towards Northstar Ski Resort and is described in the Brockway Summit to Northstar tour (no. 53). There are also two roads which head south. Of these, the western-most (right) road is the continuation of Mt. Watson Road; do not follow it. You want the easternmost (left) of the two which is a Forest Service Protection Road that intersects Mt. Watson Road just past the road to Northstar. Be aware that at least one previous road and other subsequent roads are marked as Forest Service Protection Roads.

2.6 – 4.4 –300 **(8)** Ski south on the easternmost (left) road for 1.8 miles until you reach **Watson Creek (9)**. The road descends steadily after the first level 1.1 miles.

4.4 – 5.4 –100 **(9)** Continue to descend on the road, passing a road on your right just after crossing the creek, passing a road on your left in another 0.3 mile, and a passing a road on your right a short distance farther ahead. Continue south for 0.2 mile until several roads come together. Keep to the right and continue skiing south for 0.2 mile until the road becomes very level. Ski for 0.2 mile until you reach **Fulton Crescent (10)** and the end of the tour on the east (left) side of the road. You will see houses on the east side of the road as you approach Fulton Crescent.

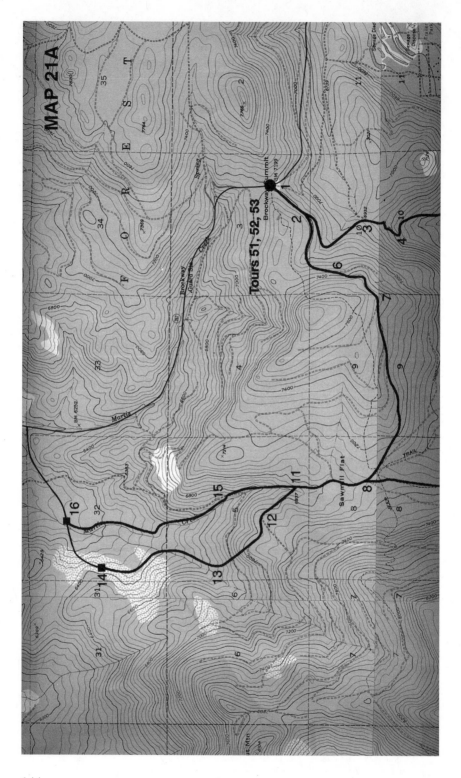

MAP 21A

FOREST

Tours 51, 52, 53

144

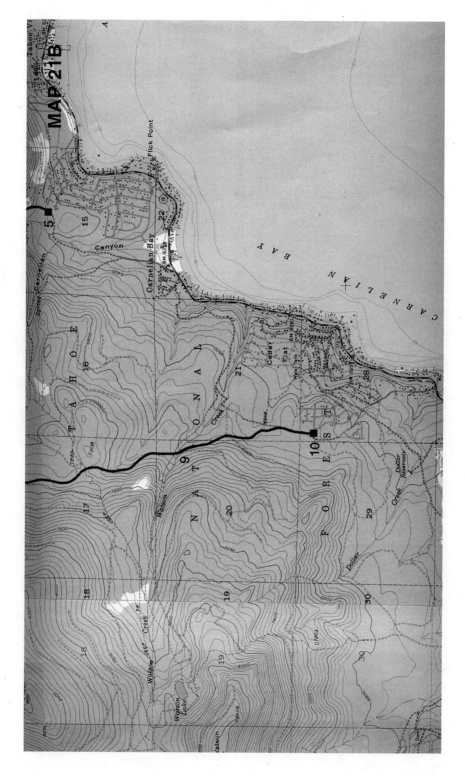

Difficulty	3
Length	5 miles one-way
Elevation	7200/+350,−1150 to Northstar Ski Resort or
	7200/+250,−1350 to West Martis Creek
Navigation	Road and map
Time	Half day
Season	December through mid-April
USGS topo	7.5' series, Martis Peak, Kings Beach
Start	Just south of Brockway Summit on Highway 267. Park in the plowed area on the west side of the highway.
End	Lodge at Northstar Ski Resort or at West Martis Creek. From Highway 267 drive 0.8 miles towards Northstar Ski Resort until you reach West Martis Creek. Park on the south (left) side of the road just east of the creek; some trash containers and a sign indicating stables may be your best landmarks. To reach the ski resort continue on the road for 0.4 mile.

This tour offers the same wonderful views of Lake Tahoe as the Brockway Summit to Tahoe City tour (no. 52). You can end this tour either at Northstar Ski Resort or at West Martis Creek. Of the two possible ending points, the tour to West Martis Creek is more difficult due to the final 1.2 miles through dense trees.

Mileage Log

0.0 – 2.6   +250,−350 **(1)** Follow the Brockway Summit to Tahoe City tour (no. 52) for 2.6 miles along Mt. Watson Road until you reach **Sawmill Flat (8)**.

2.6 – 3.1   −150 **(8)** Locate the road that descends north toward Northstar and follow it for 0.5 mile to a **dam (11)** not shown on the topo. Do not attempt to ski on the reservoir since the ice is never stable.

3.1 – 3.1   +0 **(11)** Ski directly down to or follow the road as it makes a loop until you reach a **road junction (11)** at the base of the north side of the dam.

To reach the
Northstar Ski Resort terminus

3.1 – 3.4   +100 **(11)** Follow the road that crosses West Martis Creek at the base of the dam and then climb gradually for 0.3 mile until you reach a **road junction (12)**.

3.4 – 3.8   –250 **(12)** Ski on the north (right) fork for 0.4 mile until you reach the **downhill ski slopes (13)** just above the day lodge.

3.8 – 4.9   –400 **(13)** Descend to the day lodge and then follow the easy runs for a total of 1.1 miles until you reach the **main lodge (14)**.

To reach the
West Martis Creek terminus

3.1 – 3.6   –200 **(11)** From the base of the dam, follow the road north and parallel to the creek on its east (right) side for 0.5 mile until you reach a **plowed road (15)**. This private road leads to Northstar's maintenance area and cannot be used for an ending point.

3.8 – 5.0   –650 **(15)** Cross the plowed road, descend to West Martis Creek, and then ski north along the creek for a total of 1.2 miles until you reach the **ending point (16)**.

Lake Tahoe from Mt. Watson Road

Difficulty	3
Length	8 miles round trip
Elevation	7000/+1750,−1750
Navigation	Road and map
Time	Full day
Season	December through April
USGS topo	7.5′ series, Martis Peak
Start	Highway 267, 0.5 mile north of Brockway Summit. Park in the plowed area on the east side of the road.

Ski to the top of Martis Peak if you want unbeatable views of Lake Tahoe; the summit offers the most dazzling lake views of any intermediate tour in the Lake Tahoe Basin. Once on the summit, savor both the glorious views and those tasty morsels you carried up.

Although the route to the summit of Martis Peak is now popular with snowmobilers, this tour is well worth enduring their nuisance.

Advanced skiers can incorporate the tour to Martis Peak into longer tours in the area. The one-way Martis Peak and Mt. Baldy Traverse (no. 55), which requires only a short shuttle, culminates in a descent to Kings Beach. The one-way Mt. Rose Highway to Brockway Summit tour (no. 58) requires a long shuttle, but is the most outstanding tour in the entire Lake Tahoe Basin.

Mileage Log

0.0 – 1.3 +550 **(1)** Climb steadily east on the snow-covered road for 1.3 miles until you reach a **road junction (2)**. In this first section, expect to pass several small roads as you continue on the obvious main road. At the junction, USFS Road 16N33 descends east (straight); the route continues on the road which turns north (left).

1.3 – 1.8 +100 **(2)** Turn north (left) and ski on the road for 0.5 mile until you reach a large, **flat area (3)** where several roads connect and a drainage descends southeast.

1.8 – 3.1 +700 **(3)** Climb steadily on the road which heads northeast for 1.3 miles until you reach the south ridge of Martis Peak and a **road junction (4)**. If you see any forks in the road while ascending, always continue up and to the northeast. At the junction, the road that continues to the east (straight) and then northeast is part of the Martis Peak and Mt. Baldy Traverse; this tour continues on the road to the north (left).

3.1 – 3.8 +400 **(4)** Follow the road to the north (left) for 0.6 mile and then to the southeast for 0.1 mile until you reach the **summit of**

Martis Peak (5). As an alternative, you can ascend the south ridge to the summit.

Lake Tahoe

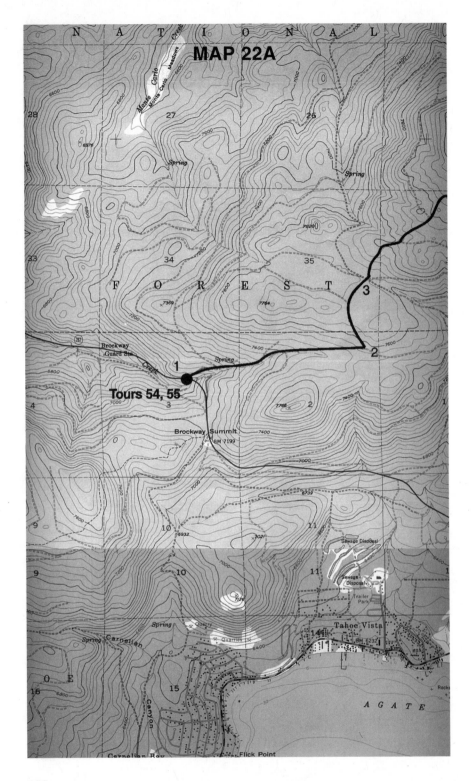

MAP 22A

Tours 54, 55

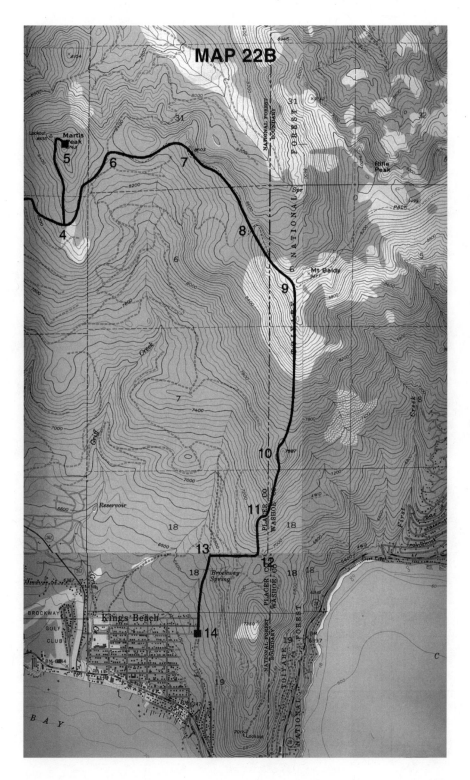

MAP 22B

151

55 Martis Peak and Mt. Baldy Traverse

MAP 22A-22B
PAGE 150-151

Difficulty	5
Length	8 miles one-way
Elevation	7000/+2150,–2650
Navigation	Road, map and compass
Time	Full day
Season	Late December through early April
USGS topo	7.5' series, Martis Peak, Mt. Rose, Kings Beach
Start	Highway 267, 0.5 mile north of Brockway Summit. Park in the plowed area on the east side of the road where the highway makes a sharp turn.
End	End of Cutthroat Avenue in Kings Beach. From Highway 28 in Kings Beach drive north on Highway 267 for 0.2 mile, turn right onto Dolly Varden Avenue, at the next intersection turn left onto Wolf, at the next intersection turn right onto Cutthroat Avenue, and drive 0.8 mile to its end.

This advanced tour, which offers spectacular views and lots of downhill, challenges even the most advanced cross-country skier. The route climbs from Brockway Summit to the saddle just east of Martis Peak, then makes a giant traverse along a ridge to Mt. Baldy, and finally drops 2500 feet to Kings Beach. The route described below does not actually pass over Martis Peak or Mt. Baldy although both can be climbed along the way.

Quite different in nature, the Mt. Rose Highway to Brockway Summit tour (no. 58), which includes a long, spectacular traverse of corniced ridges, covers much of the same terrain as this tour. However, it does not include the decent to Kings Beach.

Although the route to the summit of Martis Peak is now popular with snowmobilers, their presence decreases dramatically beyond the peak.

Mileage Log

0.0 – 3.1   +1350 **(1)** Follow the Martis Peak tour (no. 54) for 3.1 miles until you reach the south ridge of Martis Peak and a **road junction (4)**. The road to the north (left) leads to Martis Peak; this tour continues on the road to the east (straight) and then northeast.

3.1 – 3.7   +50 **(4)** Follow the road to the east (straight) and then northeast for 0.6 mile until you reach the **saddle (6)** to the east of Martis Peak.

As an alternative, you can ascend to the summit of Martis Peak and descend directly to the saddle to the east. This excursion adds 0.4 mile, a 400-foot climb, and a steep 350-foot descent through trees.

3.7 – 4.3   +200 **(6)** Ski east, traversing around the south side of a knob and then climbing, for a total of 0.6 mile until you reach **Peak 8603 (7)** which is at the northwest end of a narrow ridge that parallels the upper reaches of Juniper Creek.

4.3 – 5.0   +100 **(7)** Ski southeast along the ridge for 0.7 mile until you reach the location where the **ridge begins to climb at a very steep angle (8)**. As you ski, Lake Tahoe will appear to the south.

Along this section stay close to the ridge no matter how advantageous dropping down may seem. If you drop too low, you will have a steeper than necessary climb, or you will end up in an avalanche area southwest of Mt. Baldy.

5.0 – 5.6   +450 **(8)** Climb southeast at a very steep angle along the ridge and then gradually for a total of 0.6 mile until you reach the **south ridge of Mt. Baldy (9)**. When you reach the obvious south ridge, the summit of Mt. Baldy will be 0.1 mile to the northeast and 100 feet above. Looking south and down the ridge you can see Kings Beach.

5.6 – 6.7   –1350 **(9)** Descend south for 1.1 miles until you reach **Peak 7887 (10)**. At first the descent is gradual and the open terrain is perfect for touring. As you drop at a steeper angle, still in open terrain, be aware of avalanche danger although you are technically on a ridge.

As you descend, enjoy the views of Truckee, Donner Lake, Martis Peak, and the section you traversed earlier. Also, if you look very carefully south, you can see the overhead cables, which you will encounter later, crossing the ridge.

6.7 – 7.2   –500 **(10)** Pass Peak 7887 on its west (right) side, then continue south and descend into the trees for a total of 0.5 mile until you reach a **saddle (11)** to the north of a small knob.

7.2 – 7.5   –300 **(11)** Traverse south around the west (right) side of a small knob and continue to descend south for a total of 0.3 mile until you reach a **clearing (12)** where the previously mentioned overhead cables cross the ridge.

7.5 – 7.8   –300 **(12)** Follow the cables west and down the clearing for 0.3 mile until you reach a **road (13)** where the cables turn south (left). Part way down the clearing you may see a road heading south; do not follow it.

When planning this tour, take into consideration that this section is covered with manzanita.

55

7.8 – 8.4   –200 **(13)** Turn south (left) and follow the road south for 0.6 mile to the **ending point (14)**. Stay right at all forks in the road as you descend.

Fire lookout near Martis Peak

MAP 23
PAGE 157

Northstar to Lake Tahoe via Mt. Pluto

56

Difficulty	4
Length	7 miles one-way
Elevation	6400/+2300,–2000
Navigation	Map and compass
Time	Full day
Season	Late December through March
USGS topo	7.5' series, Martis Peak, Tahoe City, Kings Beach
Start	Northstar Ski Resort located off Highway 267 between Truckee and Kings Beach.
End	West end of Fulton Crescent in Cedar Flat. From the main intersection in Tahoe City, drive northeast on North Lake Blvd. (Highway 28) for 3.5 miles to Old County Road. Turn north onto Old County Road, drive for 0.7 mile, and turn right onto La Crosse Drive. At the tee intersection 0.3 mile ahead, turn left onto Fulton Crescent and drive 0.1 mile to its end.

The main attraction of this tour is the 1900-foot descent from the summit of Mt. Pluto to Lake Tahoe. The price you pay for the downhill run is a steep 2200-foot climb from the base of Northstar Ski Resort to the summit of Mt. Pluto.

If you are seeking ideal downhill conditions for the descent, I recommend early spring when the corn-snow can be excellent all the way down to Lake Tahoe. The tour is even better with powder snow, but you will rarely find good powder all the way down to the lake.

In past years, the ski resort has permitted cross-country skiers to pass through without comment. To maintain that the good relationship, please ski on the edge of the groomed ski slopes and only cross the slopes where absolutely necessary. At the top of the Rendezvous chairlift, where you leave the ski resort boundary, tell the lift operator that you are leaving and leave in a single file.

Mileage Log

0.0 – 0.9   +200 **(1)** Follow the Big Springs chairlift south for 0.9 mile until you reach the **day lodge (2)**.

0.9 – 2.3   +1200 **(2)** Follow the Aspen chairlift south for 1.4 miles until you reach the base of the **Comstock chairlift (3)**.

2.3 – 2.6   +200 **(3)** Climb west at a steep angle for 0.3 mile, following a ski run, not a chairlift, until you reach the north **ridge (4)** of Mt. Pluto. Northstar refers to this ridge as the West Ridge run.

2.6 – 3.2 +600 **(4)** Climb south along the ridge for 0.6 mile until you reach the **summit of Mt. Pluto (5)**.

3.2 – 3.6 –250 **(5)** Descend east on a road for 0.4 mile until you reach the top of the **Rendezvous chairlift (6)**. This is where you leave the road and the hectic alpine ski scene.

3.6 – 4.8 –550 **(6)** Descend southwest for 1.2 miles, over the best downhill terrain of the tour, until you reach the **saddle (7)** between Mt. Pluto and Mt. Watson. Savor the descent and take time to enjoy the views of Lake Tahoe as you drop through the scattered timber. Expect to cross several roads on your descent, following them only if they head in the correct direction.

4.8 – 5.3 +50,–50 **(7)** Traverse southeast along the northern slopes of Mt. Watson for 0.5 mile until you reach the southeast end of **Watson Lake (8)**. There is a road you can follow around Watson Lake.

5.3 – 5.7 +50 **(8)** Leave the road and traverse east until you reach a broad **saddle (9)** on the east ridge of Mt. Watson.

5.7 – 7.3 –1150 (9) Descend southeast through several clearings and sparsely wooded areas until you enter a gully north of a ridge; then descend the gully southeast until the terrain becomes level; then ski east for a total of 1.6 miles until you reach the **ending point (10)** at Fulton Crescent.

A short rest on the way to the summit

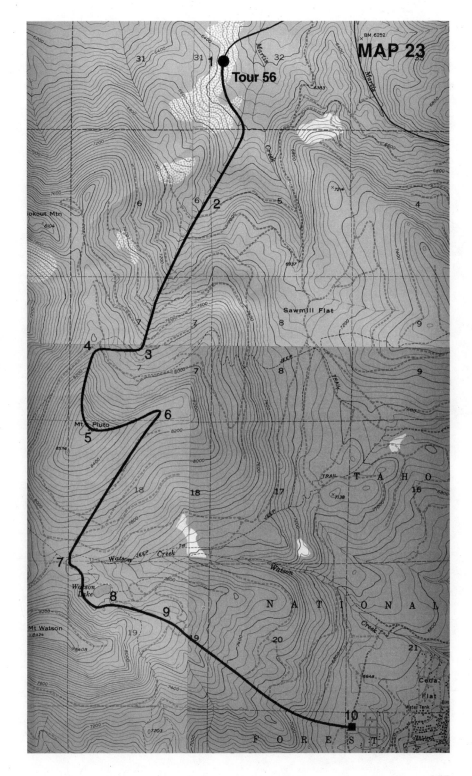

MAP 23

Tour 56

Corniced ridge on Mt. Rose Highway to Brockway Summit tour

Tahoe Meadows **57**

Difficulty	1
Length	Short
Elevation	8600/Nil
Navigation	Adjacent to road
Time	Short
Season	December through April
USGS topo	7.5' series, Mt. Rose
Start	Highway 431 (formerly 27), 7.2 miles north of Highway 28 and Incline Village, and 1.0 miles south of Mt. Rose Summit.

The relatively high altitude and the lack of vegetation make Tahoe Meadows a good choice for skiing very early in the season. The large, flat, open meadows on the south side of the highway and the bordering mild hills offer plenty of easy touring and good opportunities for beginners to master the fundaments of cross-country skiing. Across the highway and next to the road are steeper slopes for the more adventuresome.

There are several things worth noting before choosing to ski in the Tahoe Meadows area. First, the high altitude and the openness of the area make it susceptible to high winds; this can result in windpacked snow which is poor for skiing. While touring in this area, keep in mind that all the slopes in the Mt. Rose area should be considered avalanche prone. Finally, this area is very popular among snowmobilers.

58 Mt. Rose Highway to Brockway Summit

Difficulty	4
Length	11 miles one-way
Elevation	8550/+2150,−3700
Navigation	Road, map and compass
Time	Very long day
Season	Late December through mid-April
USGS topo	7.5' series, Mt. Rose, Martis Peak
Start	Highway 431 (formerly 27), 6.8 miles north of Highway 28 and Incline Village, and 1.4 miles south of Mt. Rose Summit.
End	Highway 267, 0.5 mile north of Brockway Summit. Park in the plowed area on the east side of the road.

Without doubt, this tour along windswept, corniced ridges overlooking daz-zling, blue Lake Tahoe is the pre-eminent "classic" tour in the Tahoe area. The trip starts at Tahoe Meadows on Mt. Rose Highway at 8,550 feet and ends at Brockway Summit at 7,100 feet. Ahhhhhh, a net elevation loss of 1,550 feet. Better yet, after quickly climbing to the tour's highest point, it is a rolling tour with short climbs to the several peaks that are traversed.

The ridges in this tour, which make this a classic tour, are no place to be in foul weather. Pick a fair weather day so that you can enjoy both the skiing and the views.

Mileage Log

0.0 – 0.5   −100 **(1)** Ski west and then descend for a total of 0.5 mile until you reach **Third Creek (2)**.

0.5 – 1.4   +900 **(2)** Cross Third Creek and ascend west on a broad shoulder for 0.9 mile until you reach a broad **pass (3)** located between rocky Peak 9773 and Peak 9561. These two peaks are visible from the starting point.

1.4 – 2.0   −50 **(3)** Traverse around the south side of Peak 9773 and then descend for a total of 0.6 mile until you reach a location north and above **Mud Lake (4)**. Start the traverse very close to Peak 9773. There is a sign pointing up the peak at Sullivan Chute — definitely only for crazies. Be aware that the traverse is across a steep slope that is not safe when icy or when snow conditions are unstable.

2.0 – 2.3   +400 **(4)** Climb south onto a ridge and then ascend the ridge north-west for a total of 0.3 mile until you reach **Rose Knob Peak (5)**.

160

2.3 – 3.7	+400,–500 **(5)** Ski west along a ridge for 1.4 miles until you reach **Rose Knob (6)**.
3.7 – 4.3	+100,–300 **(6)** Ski southwest along a ridge, past Peak 9499, for 0.6 mile until you reach the location where the **ridge forks (7)**. Rifle Peak is nearby to the north.
4.3 – 5.1	–150 **(7)** Ski along the ridge that heads southwest (left fork) for 0.8 mile until you reach **Mt. Baldy (8)**.
5.1 – 6.5	–850 **(8)** Descend southwest along the ridge for 0.1 mile, then descend northwest (right) along the ridge for 1.3 miles until you reach the east side of a small **knob (9)**.
6.5 – 7.0	+0 **(9)** Ski around the south side of the knob for 0.5 mile until you reach a **saddle (10)** to the east of Martis Peak.
7.0 – 7.3	+350 **(10)** Climb west at a steep angle for 0.3 mile to the **summit of Martis Peak (11)**. You can traverse south and intersect Martis Peak's south ridge and the route at (12) if you are running short of time or energy.
7.3 – 8.0	–400 **(11)** Descend north on a road for 0.1 mile and then south on the road for 0.6 mile until you reach a **road junction (12)** on Martis Peak's south ridge.
8.0 – 9.3	–700 **(12)** Turn west (right) and follow the road for 1.3 miles until you reach a **flat area (13)** where several roads connect and a drainage descends southeast.
9.3 – 9.8	–100 **(13)** Continue to follow the road for 0.5 mile as it curves until you reach a **road junction (14)**.
9.8 – 11.1	–550 **(14)** Turn west (sharp right) and descend on the road for 1.3 miles until you reach the **ending point (15)**.

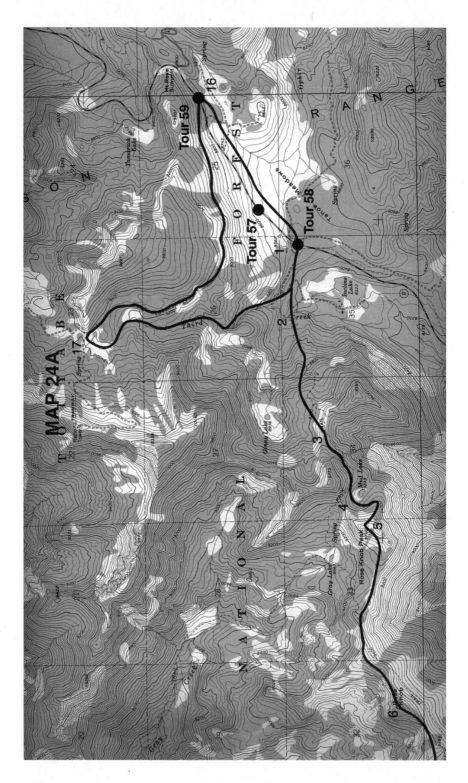

MAP 24A

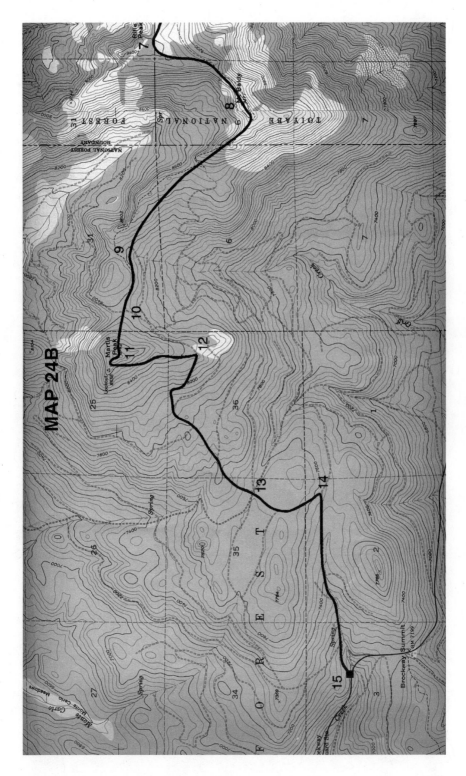

MAP 24B

163

Traverse below spectacular ridge

Third Creek Loop **59**

Difficulty	3
Length	6 miles round trip
Elevation	8850/+850,−850
Navigation	Road and map
Time	Half day
Season	December through April
USGS topo	7.5′ series, Mt. Rose
Start	Highway 431 (formerly 27), 7.9 miles north of Highway 28 and Incline Village, and 0.3 miles south of Mt. Rose Summit. A road and building are located on the north side of the highway.

Ski touring in the Mt. Rose area has good and bad points. Its high altitude makes it a good choice for anxious tourers who want to ski at the first falling of snow. If you belong to this category of skiers, you should also consider the Tahoe Meadows tour. Unfortunately, cold, windy weather plagues this rugged area where navigation is difficult, avalanche danger is considerable, and good ski touring terrain is limited. Regardless of these conditions, the loop described below offers good intermediate terrain.

Mileage Log

0.0 – 2.4 +550 **(16)** Ski west on the snow-covered road, which gradually turns north into a canyon, for 2.4 miles until you reach a **saddle (17)** and the highest point of the tour. Beyond, the road continues across very steep and dangerous terrain to the Mt. Rose Relay Station. Mt. Rose with its steep slopes is to the north.

2.4 – 4.3 −850 **(17)** Descend south along Third Creek for 1.5 miles; then turn east (there is no landmark) and ski 0.4 mile until you reach the **highway (1)** at the southwest end of Tahoe Meadows.

4.3 – 5.5 +300 **(1)** Cross to the southeast (opposite) side of the highway, and ski northeast and gradually uphill for 1.2 miles until you reach the **starting point (16)**.

60 Tahoe Meadows to Incline

MAP 25
PAGE 167

Difficulty	4
Length	4 miles one-way
Elevation	8550/+200,–1850
Navigation	Map and compass
Time	Most of a day
Season	January through March
USGS topo	7.5′ series, Mt. Rose
Start	Highway 431 (formerly 27), 6.8 miles north of Highway 28 and Incline Village, and 1.4 miles south of Mt. Rose Summit.
End	Diamond Peak Ski Resort at Incline Village.

This 1850-foot descent, nearly all in the confines of a narrow drainage, is for skiers with excellent control, that is, a good telemark turn. This tour is highly dependent on good snow conditions. The ideal time for this tour is during a cold, mild storm when you can expect good snow conditions from the start to the end.

Mileage Log

0.0 – 0.7 +100 **(1)** Ski south across Tahoe Meadows and then ascend gradually south for a total of 0.7 mile until you reach the top of a small **ridge (2)**.

0.7 – 1.2 +100 **(2)** Climb east (left) until the terrain becomes more level and then traverse southeast for a total of 0.5 mile until you reach a small **spur ridge (3)**. The tour descends the drainage located to the southeast of the spur ridge.

1.2 – 2.2 –850 **(3)** Descend southeast into the drainage and then descend the drainage for a total of 1.0 mile until you reach a location where the **drainage drops abruptly (4)**.

2.2 – 3.7 –1000 **(4)** Descend the steep section of the drainage and then follow it for a total of 1.5 miles until you reach the start of the **housing development (5)** adjacent to Diamond Peak Ski Resort.

3.7 – 3.9 +0 **(5)** Continue skiing along the creek; find a place to access a plowed road (probably Tyrol Road); then walk down it for a total of 0.2 mile until you reach the **ski resort (6)**.

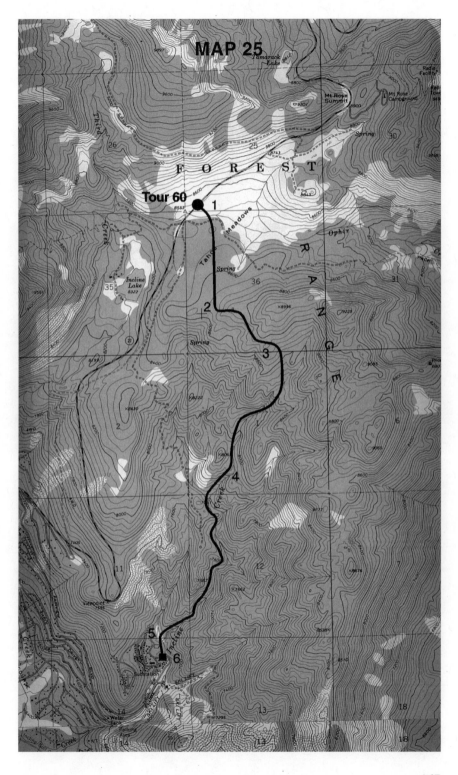

Angora Lookout

South Tahoe

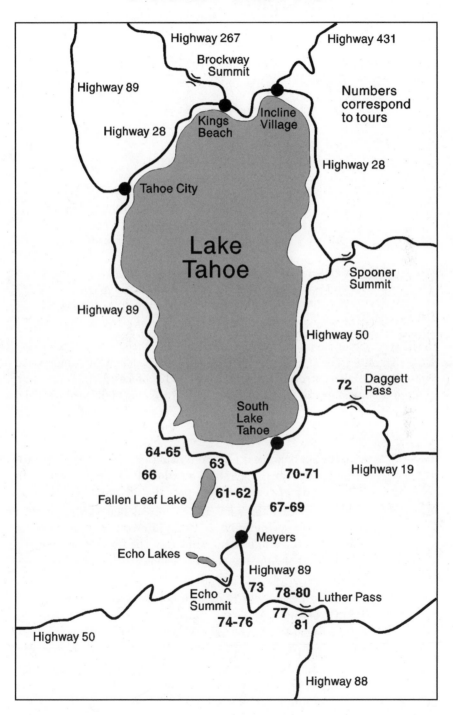

Highway 267

Brockway
Summit

Highway 431

Highway 89

Numbers
correspond
to tours

Kings
Beach

Incline
Village

Highway 28

Highway 28

Tahoe City

Lake
Tahoe

Spooner
Summit

Highway 89

Highway 50

72 Daggett
Pass

South
Lake
Tahoe

64-65

63

66

70-71

Highway 19

Fallen Leaf Lake

61-62

67-69

Echo Lakes

Meyers

Highway 89

73

78-80

Luther Pass

Echo
Summit

77

74-76

81

Highway 50

Highway 88

Difficulty	3
Length	4 miles round trip to lookout and 7 miles round trip to the lakes
Elevation	6700/+700,–700 to the lookout and 6700/+1100,–1100 to the lakes
Navigation	Road
Time	Half to most of a day
Season	Mid-December through mid-April
USGS topo	7.5′ series, Emerald Bay
Start	From the intersection of Highways 50 and 89 in South Lake Tahoe, drive southwest on Lake Tahoe Blvd. for 2.7 miles and turn right onto Tahoe Mountain Road. Drive 1.1 miles and turn right onto Glenmore Way and then immediately left onto Dundee Circle. In 0.1 mile turn left onto Tahoe Mountain Road once again and park. Do not drive down the narrow plowed portion of Tahoe Mountain Road which is just ahead.

Of the spectacular panorama from Angora Lookout, the most striking feature is the rich blue color of Fallen Leaf Lake and Lake Tahoe. Other impressive sights include: the Carson Range to the east and southeast; Mt. Tallac with its steep eastern slopes to the northwest; and Lake Valley to the southeast and below.

Mileage Log

0.0 – 0.1   –50 **(1)** Ski or walk if plowed down Tahoe Mountain Road for 0.1 mile until you reach a small **meadow (2)**, located on the south (left) side of the road, which is partially obscured by trees.

0.1 – 1.8   +650 **(2)** Locate the snow-covered road that skirts the west (right) side of the meadow, and ski southwest on it for 1.7 miles until you reach **Angora Lookout (3)**. The first 0.5 mile on the road is level and the remaining 1.2 miles climbs steadily to the lookout.

To continue to Angora Lakes

1.8 – 2.5   +0 **(3)** Ski southwest on the ridge and road for 0.7 mile until you reach a **turn (4)** to the south (left) where the road begins to drop.

2.5 – 3.5   +300,–100 **(4)** Follow the road as it descends and then climbs for a total of 1.0 mile until you reach **Angora Lakes (5)**. If the road becomes too difficult to follow at its lowest point, head south and follow the power lines to the lakes.

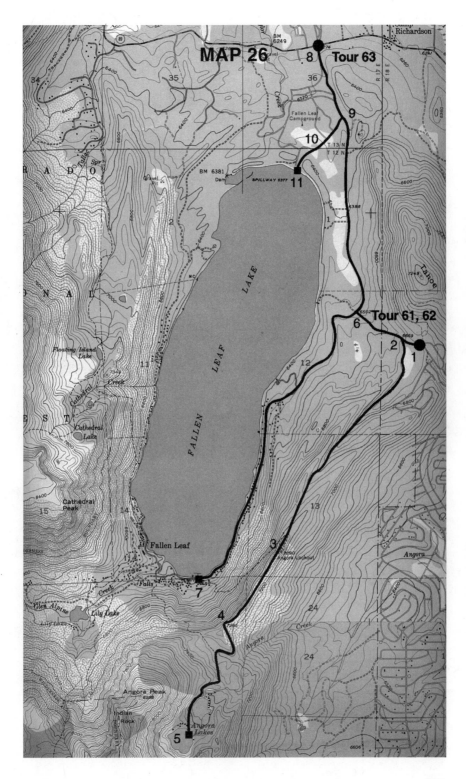

MAP 26
PAGE 171

62 Fallen Leaf Lake from Tahoe Mountain Road

Difficulty	2
Length	Up to 6 miles round trip
Elevation	6700/+400,–400
Navigation	Road
Time	Short to half day
Season	Late December through March
USGS topo	7.5′ series, Emerald Bay
Start	From the intersection of Highways 50 and 89 in South Lake Tahoe, drive southwest on Lake Tahoe Blvd. for 2.7 miles and turn right onto Tahoe Mountain Road. Drive 1.1 miles and turn right onto Glenmore Way and then immediately left onto Dundee Circle. In 0.1 mile turn left onto Tahoe Mountain Road once again and park. Do not drive down the narrow plowed portion of Tahoe Mountain Road which is just ahead.

The Tahoe Mountain Road access to Fallen Leaf Lake greatly shortens the tour to the south end of the lake as compared to the Fallen Leaf Lake from Highway 89 tour (no. 63). From the south end of the lake the view north across its 3-mile length is serene when the surface is glassy.

Along the lake there are cabins and the owners use snowmobiles to access them; to a lesser degree other snowmobilers use Fallen Leaf Lake Road. Still, many skiers will find this setting attractive; it offers a good opportunity to kick up your heels and let loose.

Keep in mind that this tour would be rated 1 in difficulty except for the first 0.5 mile which descends 300 feet. Novice skiers desiring to ski Fallen Leaf Lake from this starting point can walk down the "edge" of the road if necessary.

Mileage Log

0.0 – 0.1 –50 **(1)** Ski or walk if plowed down Tahoe Mountain Road for 0.1 mile until you reach a small **meadow (2)**, located on the south (left) side of the road, which is partially obscured by trees. The snow-covered road on the west (right) side of the meadow leads to Angora Lookout and Angora Lakes (no. 61).

0.1 – 0.5 –250 **(2)** Continue down the extension of Tahoe Mountain Road for 0.4 mile until you reach **Fallen Leaf Lake Road (6)**. A turn to the north (right) will take you to Highway 89; this tour continues to the south (left).

0.5 – 3.0 –100 **(6)** Turn south (left) onto Fallen Leaf Lake Road and ski for 2.5 miles until you reach the **south end of the lake (7)**.

MAP 26
PAGE 171

Fallen Leaf Lake from Highway 89

63

Difficulty	1 – 2
Length	2 to 9 miles round trip
Elevation	6300/+50,–50 to north end of lake or 6300/+300,–300 to south end of lake
Navigation	Road and map
Time	Few hours to full day
Season	Late December through March
USGS topo	7.5' series, Emerald Bay
Start	Intersection of Fallen Leaf Lake Road and Highway 89, 3.0 miles northwest of the intersection of Highways 50 and 89 in South Lake Tahoe, and 0.5 mile west of Camp Richardson.

No matter how far you choose to ski on Fallen Leaf Lake Road, the tour along Fallen Leaf Lake is an easy one. Created by glacial movement, the three-mile-long lake offers beginners the opportunity to ski without anxiety of significant elevation changes.

Fallen Leaf Lake Road is subject to extreme variations in snow conditions due to its low elevation and its use by snowmobilers. Pick a time when the snow cover is good. The alternate route to Fallen Leaf Lake from Tahoe Mountain Road (no. 62) tends to minimize the worst of the snow conditions because it eliminates the lowest part of this tour which is unprotected from the winter sun.

Mileage Log

0.0 – 0.5 +50 **(8)** Ski south on Fallen Leaf Lake Road for 0.5 mile until you reach a **road junction (9)**. The short route to the lake takes the west (right) fork which enters Fallen Leaf Campground. The long route takes the east (left) fork.

To continue on the short route

0.5 – 0.8 +0 **(9)** Follow the west (right) fork into the campground for 0.3 mile until you reach the edge of a large **meadow (10)**.

0.8 – 1.0 +0 **(10)** Leave the road and ski southwest for 0.2 mile over a small rise until you reach **Fallen Leaf Lake (11)**.

To continue on the long route

0.5 – 2.0 +150 **(9)** Follow the east (left) fork south for 1.5 miles until you reach **Tahoe Mountain Road (6)**.

2.0 – 4.5 –100 **(6)** Continue south (straight) on Fallen Leaf Lake Road for 2.5 miles until you reach the **south end of the lake (7)**.

64 Mt. Tallac Direct

Difficulty	5
Length	4 miles round trip
Elevation	6500/+3250,–3250
Navigation	Map
Time	Full day
Season	March and April
USGS topo	7.5′ series, Emerald Bay
Start	From the intersection of Highways 50 and 89 in South Lake Tahoe, drive 4.9 miles northwest on Highway 89 to Spring Creek Road and turn southwest (left) onto it. Drive 0.7 mile, turn right onto Pomo Road, and continue for 0.3 mile to the starting point. You will need to park earlier if the road conditions are poor.

This route is a favorite of Tahoe's ski randonnee crowd; on occasion downhill skiers endure carrying their skis to the summit for the pleasure of the grand descent — more than 3000 feet in less than 2 miles.

This tour follows the most direct route to the summit of Mt. Tallac. It ascends the mountain's northeast bowl and potential avalanche path. Therefore, it should only be attempted when conditions are known to be stable. The more traditional route to the summit of Mt. Tallac (no. 65), along its north ridge, offers considerable more security until you reach its upper north slope.

An interesting one-way tour can be created by ascending Mt. Tallac by either the direct route or the north ridge route, and descending south to Fallen Leaf Lake (no. 66); in effect, you cross Mt. Tallac.

Mileage Log

0.0 – 1.4 +2700 **(1)** Climb south and then southwest, working your way into and up a bowl, for a total of 1.4 miles until you reach the north **ridge (2)** of Mt. Tallac.

1.4 – 1.6 +100 **(2)** Ski south along the ridge for 0.2 mile until you reach the **bowl (3)** on Mt. Tallac's the north slope.

1.6 – 1.7 +300 **(3)** Ski into and up the bowl for 0.1 mile until you reach the small **saddle (4)** to the northwest (right) of Mt. Tallac.

1.7 – 1.8 +150 **(4)** Ski around to and up the south slope of Mt. Tallac until you reach its **summit (5)**.

Mt. Tallac's North Ridge **65**

Difficulty	5
Length	5 miles round trip
Elevation	6400/+3350,−3350
Navigation	Map
Time	Full day
Season	March and April
USGS topo	7.5′ series, Emerald Bay
Start	From the intersection of Highways 50 and 89 in South Lake Tahoe, drive 4.9 miles northwest on Highway 89 to Spring Creek Road and turn southwest (left) onto it. Drive 0.4 mile, turn right onto Mattole Road, and continue for 0.4 mile to the starting point. You will need to park earlier if the road conditions are poor.

The satisfaction of meeting the challenge and an unparalleled view of Lake Tahoe, Desolation Wilderness and the Crystal Range are the rewards of this extremely demanding ascent of Mt. Tallac. Although the total distance is short, this very steep tour requires an early start.

Although this route to the summit of Mt. Tallac is safer than the direct route (no. 64), the north slope near the summit of the mountain which can not be avoided and the bowls to the northeast of the summit are severely avalanche prone. Therefore, this tour should not be attempted when conditions are unstable.

Skiers desiring to climb Mt. Tallac, but not for the thrill of the steep descent, will find a descent via Mt. Tallac's south side an interesting alternative (no. 66).

Mileage Log

0.0 – 0.5 +550 **(6)** Climb northwest until you reach the north **ridge (7)** of Mt. Tallac where you can see Cascade Lake to the north.

0.5 – 2.4 +2350 **(7)** Ascend south along the north ridge for 1.9 miles until you reach the **bowl (3)** on Mt. Tallac's the north slope.

2.4 – 2.5 +300 **(3)** Ski into and up the bowl for 0.1 mile until you reach the small **saddle (4)** to the northwest (right) of Mt. Tallac.

2.5 – 2.6 +150 **(4)** Ski around to and up the south slope of Mt. Tallac until you reach its **summit (5)**.

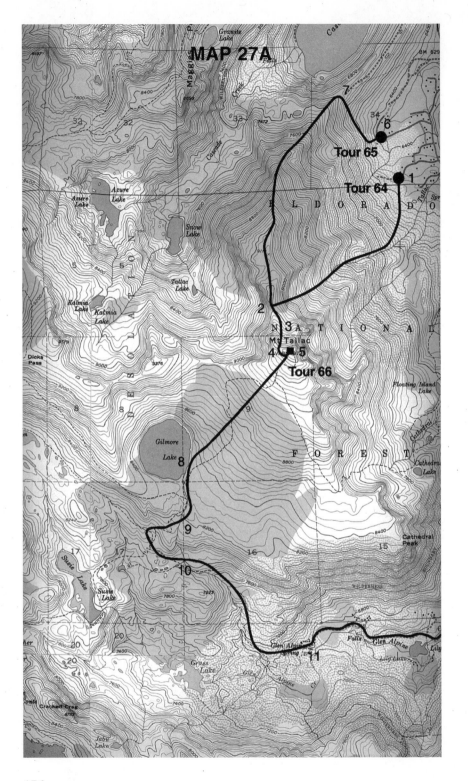

MAP 27A

Tour 65

Tour 64

Tour 66

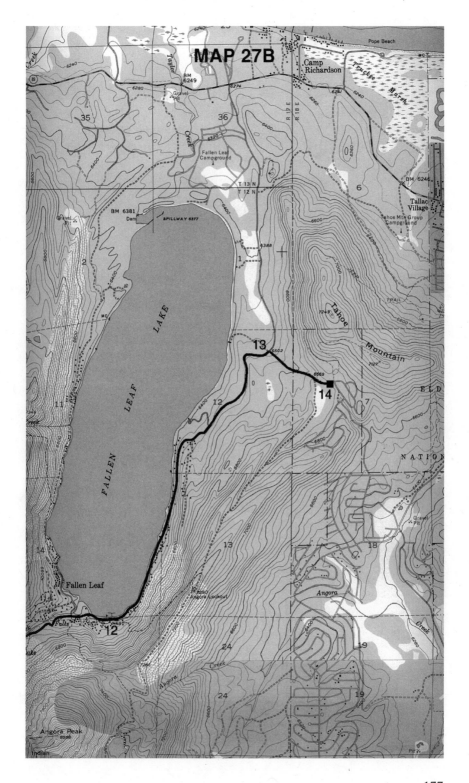

MAP 27B

177

66 Mt. Tallac to Fallen Leaf Lake

Difficulty	5
Length	8 miles one-way (plus distance to reach Mt. Tallac)
Elevation	9750/+300,–3350 (plus elevation gain to reach Mt. Tallac)
Navigation	Road, map and compass
Time	Very long day (includes time to reach Mt. Tallac)
Season	March and April
USGS topo	7.5′ series, Emerald Bay, Fallen Leaf Lake
Start	Summit of Mt. Tallac (see tours 64 and 65).
End	From the intersection of Highways 50 and 89 in South Lake Tahoe, drive southwest on Lake Tahoe Blvd. for 2.7 miles and turn right onto Tahoe Mountain Road. Drive 1.1 miles and turn right onto Glenmore Way and then immediately left onto Dundee Circle. In 0.1 mile turn left onto Tahoe Mountain Road once again and park. Do not drive down the narrow plowed portion of Tahoe Mountain Road which is just ahead.

This descent from the summit of Mt. Tallac is an alternative to the very steep routes (nos. 64 and 65) normally used to ascend the mountain. It offers a wide-open, modestly steep, 1450-foot descent to Gilmore Lake. Beyond Gilmore Lake you must pick your way down to Glen Alpine Spring. Then it is a five-mile ski on roads to the end of the tour.

Mileage Log

0.0 – 1.1   –1450 **(5)** From the summit of Mt. Tallac descend southwest for 1.1 miles until you reach **Gilmore Lake (8)**.

1.1 – 1.4   –100 **(8)** Ski south along the east (left) side of Gilmore Lake's outlet creek for 0.3 mile until you reach the approximate location where the **summer trail crosses the creek (9)**.

1.4 – 2.1   –400 **(9)** Cross the creek and descend, making a loop, for a total of 0.7 mile until you reach the **creek (10)** once again.

2.1 – 3.3   –1000 **(10)** Cross the creek and descend, southeast and then east, along the north (left) side of the creek for a total of 1.2 miles until you reach the cabin at **Glen Alpine Spring (11)**.

> *At Glen Alpine Spring you must locate the road that heads east.*

3.3 – 5.2   –400 **(11)** Descend east on the road for 1.9 miles until you reach the south end of **Fallen Leaf Lake (12)**.

5.2 – 7.7 +100 **(12)** Ski north along the east side of Fallen Leaf Lake for 2.5 miles until you reach the junction with **Tahoe Mountain Road (13)**.

7.7 – 8.2 +200 **(13)** Turn east (right) onto Tahoe Mountain Road and climb for 0.5 mile until you reach the **ending point (14)** at Dundee Circle.

It doesn't get any better   by Joan Lindberg

67 Fountain Place

Difficulty	3
Length	9 miles round trip
Elevation	6400/+1400,−1400
Navigation	Road
Time	Full day
Season	Late December through early April
USGS topo	7.5′ series, Freel Peak
Start	Corner of Oneidas Street and Chibcha in Meyers. From Highway 50 in Meyers follow Pioneer Trail northeast for 0.9 mile. Turn right onto Oneidas Street and Chibcha is 0.2 mile ahead.

The tour to Fountain Place allows you to ski all day without the worry of navigating because it follows roads the entire way. The meadow at Fountain Place is a perfect setting for lunch. Freel Peak, the highest peak in the Lake Tahoe Basin, is nearby to the east.

Mileage Log

0.0 – 0.5 +100 **(1)** Ski on the snow-covered continuation of Oneidas Street for 0.5 mile until you reach a road junction; take the fork to the east (right) and immediately reach **Saxon Creek (2)**. There is a bridge across the creek.

0.5 – 2.2 +450 **(2)** Cross the creek and ski on the road for 1.7 miles until you reach **road junction (3)**.

2.2 – 2.3 +0 **(3)** Take the east (left) fork and ski for 0.1 mile until you cross **Trout Creek (4)** on a bridge.

2.3 – 2.6 +150 **(4)** Continue on the road for 0.3 mile until you reach a **180-degree right turn (5)**.

2.6 – 4.6 +700 **(5)** Ski on the road for 2.0 miles until you reach Fountain Place and the large **meadow (6)** beyond. In the first 1.0 mile of this section you ascend at a steep angle; exercise caution immediately after heavy snowfalls and when other avalanche conditions exist. In the second 1.0 mile you ascend more gradually.

Freel Peak **68**

Difficulty	5
Length	14 miles round trip
Elevation	6400/+4500,−4500
Navigation	Road and map
Time	Very long day
Season	March through early April
USGS topo	7.5′ series, Freel Peak
Start	Corner of Oneidas Street and Chibcha in Meyers. From Highway 50 in Meyers follow Pioneer Trail northeast for 0.9 mile. Turn right onto Oneidas Street and Chibcha is 0.2 mile ahead.

The view from Freel Peak, the highest point in the Lake Tahoe area, is dramatic. This extremely demanding one-day tour should only be attempted by the very strongest skiers. Because the avalanche danger on this tour is extreme, do not attempt it after a heavy snowfall or when other unstable conditions exist.

Mileage Log

0.0 – 4.6 +1400 **(1)** Follow the Fountain Place tour (no. 67) for 4.6 miles until you reach the **meadow (6)** adjacent to Fountain Place.

4.6 – 6.1 +1900 **(6)** Climb up a gully to the northeast for 1.5 miles until you reach the **saddle (7)** between Freel Peak and Peak 9885. The saddle separates Fountain Place and High Meadows.

6.1 – 6.7 +1000 **(7)** Climb southeast up a ridge for 0.6 mile until you reach an **east-west ridge (8)**.

6.7 – 7.0 +200 **(8)** Ski east on the ridge for 0.3 mile until you reach the **summit of Freel Peak (9)** next to the microwave station.

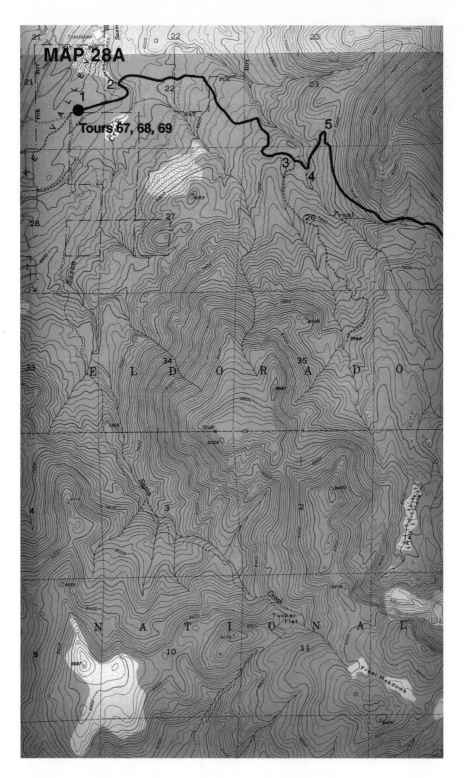

MAP 28A

Tours 67, 68, 69

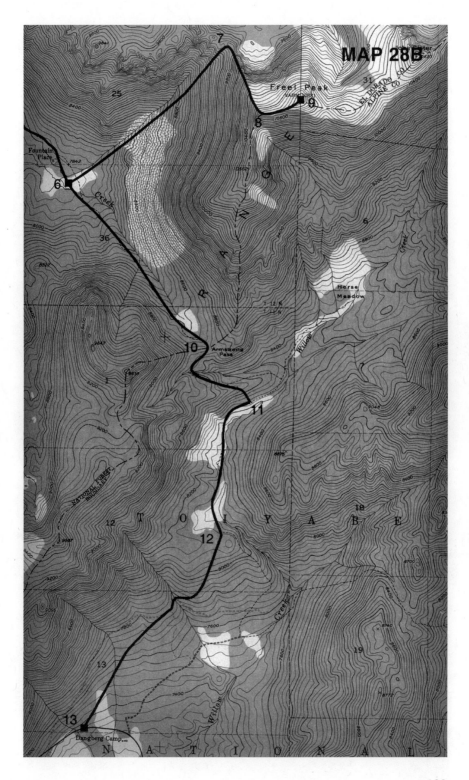

MAP 28B

183

Difficulty	4
Length	10 miles one-way
Elevation	6400/+2300,–1200
Navigation	Road and map
Time	Full day
Season	Late December through early April
USGS topo	7.5′ series, Freel Peak
Start	Corner of Oneidas Street and Chibcha in Meyers. From Highway 50 in Meyers follow Pioneer Trail northeast for 0.9 mile. Turn right onto Oneidas Street and Chibcha is 0.2 mile ahead.
End	Highway 89, 1.0 mile east of Luther Pass and 1.8 miles north of Picketts Junction (junction of Highways 88 and 89). There is a turnout on the south side of the highway.

This delightful advanced-intermediate tour is an excellent choice for intermediate skiers who want to get a taste of longer tours. Although part of the tour is cross-country, it is in a very well-defined drainage or elsewhere where navigation is not difficult.

The tour starts with a gradual climb on roads to Fountain Place. The cross-country that follows is up a drainage to Armstrong Pass and then a short descent off the pass. The last stretch is a gentle glide down a road to the end of the tour.

Mileage Log

0.0 – 4.6 +1400 **(1)** Follow the Fountain Place tour (no. 67) for 4.6 miles to the **meadow (6)** adjacent to Fountain Place.

4.6 – 6.2 +900 **(6)** Ski southeast up a distinct drainage for 1.6 miles until you reach **Armstrong Pass (10)**. The skiing is in general easier on the southwest (right) side of the creek though you may find yourself crossing back and forth. Be cautious when crossing on snowbridges.

6.2 – 6.8 –350 **(10)** Zig-zag to the southeast for 0.6 mile until you reach **Willow Creek (11)**.

6.8 – 7.9 –100 **(11)** Ski south along Willow Creek for 1.1 miles until you reach a relative **flat, open area (12)**.

7.9 – 9.6 –750 **(12)** Ski southwest, picking up a road somewhere along the way, for 1.7 miles until you reach the **ending point (13)**.

Both skiing and navigation are easy along this creek

70 High Meadows

70 High Meadows

MAP 29
PAGE 188

Difficulty	3
Length	7 miles round trip
Elevation	6550/+1600,–1600
Navigation	Road
Time	Most of day
Season	Late December through early April
USGS topo	7.5′ series, South Lake Tahoe
Start	End of High Meadows Trail in South Lake Tahoe. High Meadows Trail intersects Pioneer Trail 4.8 miles north of Highway 50 in Meyers and 2.6 miles south of Ski Run Blvd. in South Lake Tahoe. The end of High Meadows Trail is 0.8 mile south of Pioneer Trail.

This tour climbs steadily to a high point overlooking the basin in which High Meadows is located. Beyond, it is a short descent to the meadows itself. Along part of the route there are good views of the mountains to the northwest.

Mileage Log

0.0 – 1.0 +200 **(1)** Ski east on the snow-covered road for 1.0 mile until you reach a locked **gate (2)** where a sign reads: "Be a good neighbor. Respect the land. Pack it in — pack it out. Private property. No vehicles. Trimmer Cattle Ranch." From this sign and given that the caretaker has not indicated that cross-country skiers are not welcome, it appears to be okay for skiers to proceed. Do not damage the fence or the gate if you must climb over either, and respect all requests of the owner or caretaker.

1.0 – 1.7 +250,–100 **(2)** Continue on the road, climbing and then descending, for a total of 0.7 mile until you reach a **creek (3)** which you must cross carefully.

1.7 – 2.0 +300 **(3)** Climb along the road, which is steeper now, for 0.3 mile until you reach some power lines and just ahead a **fork in the road (4)**.

2.0 – 3.0 +650 **(4)** Follow the north (left) fork and continue to climb along the road for 1.0 mile until you reach the open **high point (5)** above High Meadows. If you lose the road as you are climbing, pick your own route to the east until you reach the high point.

3.0 – 3.4 –100 **(5)** Turn north (left) and ski a total of 0.4 mile; first on a level and open course until you reach the power lines again and then descending along the power lines to the north end of **High Meadows (6)**.

On your return trip, you may want to leave the road to enjoy a descent on the sparsely wooded terrain just below the high point. Farther down, if the descent on the fast road becomes too difficult, ski off and parallel to it.

Star Lake

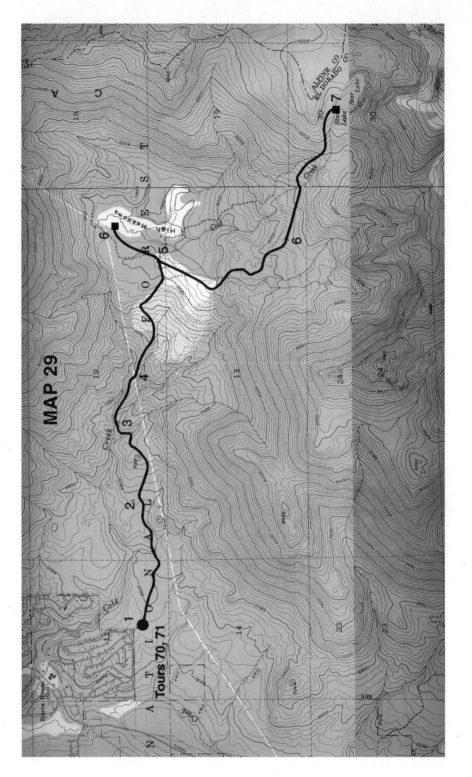

MAP 29

Tours 70, 71

MAP 29
PAGE 188

Star Lake **71**

Difficulty	5
Length	10 miles round trip
Elevation	6550/+2750,−2750
Navigation	Road, map and compass
Time	Full day
Season	Late December through early April
USGS topo	7.5′ series, South Lake Tahoe, Freel Peak
Start	End of High Meadows Trail in South Lake Tahoe. High Meadows Trail intersects Pioneer Trail 4.8 miles north of Highway 50 in Meyers and 2.6 miles south of Ski Run Blvd. in South Lake Tahoe. The end of High Meadows Trail is 0.8 mile south of Pioneer Trail.

On this tour to Star Lake, located at the base of and 1700 feet below Jobs Sister, expect a steep climb and a wonderful descent. Before you begin, keep in mind that this tour traverses many steep, potentially dangerous slopes, that the route-finding can be tricky, and that snow conditions improve as you go higher.

Mileage Log

0.0 – 3.0   +1400,−100 **(1)** Follow the High Meadows tour (no. 70) for 3.0 miles until you reach the **high point (5)** above the meadows.

3.0 – 4.1   +450 **(5)** Ski south along a ridge, picking up a road, and climb for a total of 1.1 miles until you reach the **end of the road (6)**. Do not be surprised if it is difficult to follow the road. If you loose it, just continue to climb south to an elevation of about the 8200 feet where the terrain in more level.

4.1 – 5.2   +800 **(6)** Ski east until you reach Cold Creek and then ascend parallel to the creek for a total of 1.1 miles until you reach **Star Lake (7)**. You can ski on either side of the creek.

72 Kingsbury Grade to Spooner Junction

MAP 30A-30B
PAGE 192-193

Difficulty	4
Length	10 miles one-way
Elevation	7750/+1400,–2150
Navigation	Road, marked trail, map and compass
Time	Full day
Season	Late December through mid-April
USGS topo	7.5' series, South Lake Tahoe, Glenbrook
Start	End of Andria Drive in Chalet Village. From South Lake Tahoe, drive east on Highway 19 (Kingsbury Grade) for 3.0 miles and turn north onto North Benjamin Drive. North Benjamin Drive turns into Andria Drive and 1.9 miles from the highway the plowed road ends.
End	Spooner Junction Maintenance Station, 0.3 mile south of the junction of Highway 50 and 28.

Although snowmobilers frequent this area on weekends, this one-way tour from Kingsbury Grade to Spooner Junction offers a sense of remoteness and fantastic views of Lake Tahoe to the west, Jacks Valley to the east, and beautiful high peaks.

Most of this route is marked with yellow diamonds. However, the road will be difficult to follow in places and you may encountered road junctions not described here. Consult your map and compass; if in doubt head north.

Mileage Log

0.0 – 0.4 +150 **(1)** Climb north on the snow-covered road for 0.4 mile until you reach a **road junction (2)**.

0.4 – 0.5 +100 **(2)** Take the fork that makes a sharp turn to the west (left) and climb for 0.1 mile until you reach a **saddle (3)**. Enjoy the superb views to the south of the higher peaks of the Lake Tahoe Basin: East and Monument peaks, Jobs Sister, and Jobs Peak.

0.5 – 1.2 +300 **(3)** Ski north on the road for 0.7 mile until you reach a **saddle (4)** to the east of Peak 8411. Enjoy more superb views, this time to the west of Lake Tahoe, and Mt. Tallac and Pyramid Peak bordering Desolation Valley.

1.2 – 3.8 +500,–350 **(4)** Ski north for 2.6 miles until you reach a flat area near the **head of Sierra Canyon (5)**. Although there is a road this entire distance, you will likely loose it along the way. If so, ski north, picking the easiest route, until you pick up Genoa Peak Road in the gully northwest of Peak 8863.

3.8 – 4.7 +150 (**5**) Follow the road north for 0.9 mile until you reach the **saddle** (**6**) between Genoa and South Camp peaks.

4.7 – 5.3 +150 (**6**) Ski north on the road, if possible, for 0.6 mile until you reach a location **close to the highest summit of South Camp Peak** (**7**). While the top of South Camp Peak is slightly off the route, the summit is easy to reach and is a perfect lunch spot from which to enjoy the magnificent view to the east.

> *You must now locate the road if you are not on it. From the east side of South Camp Peak's highest summit, descend east into the trees and look for yellow diamond markers and the road cut. Once you find the road, you should have no trouble following it for the remainder of the tour.*

5.3 – 7.9 –1050 (**7**) Ski north on the road for 2.6 miles until you reach a **road junction** (**8**).

7.9 – 8.2 +50 (**8**) Continue on the road to the west (straight) for 0.3 mile until you reach a **saddle** (**9**) northeast of Peak 7819.

8.2 – 8.8 –400 (**9**) Descend to the northwest on the road at a steep angle for 0.6 mile until you reach a **road junction** (**10**).

8.8 – 9.7 –350 (**10**) Descend northwest (left) on the road for 0.9 mile until you reach the **ending point** (**11**) at Spooner Junction Maintenance Station.

The track will be fast on the way down

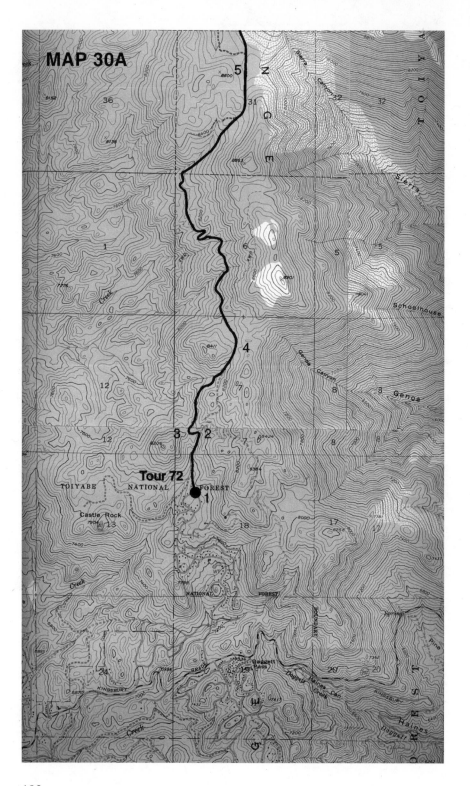

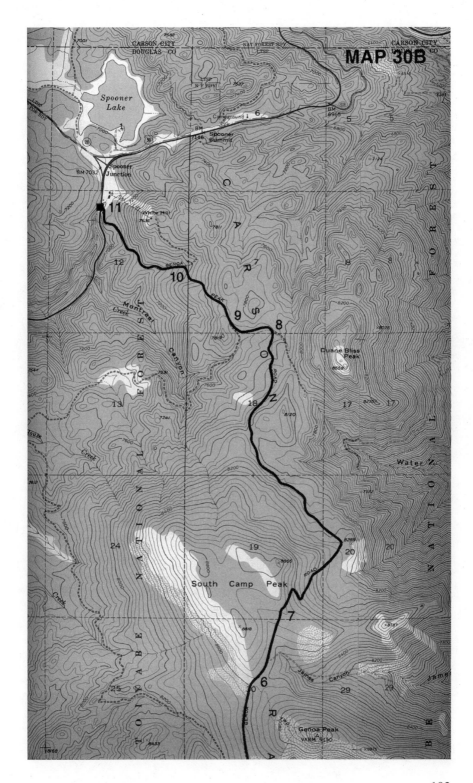

73 Government Meadow

MAP 31
PAGE 197

Difficulty	1
Length	Short
Elevation	7000/Nil
Navigation	Adjacent to plowed road
Time	Short
Season	Mid-December through mid-April
USGS topo	7.5' series, Echo Lake, Freel Peak
Start	From Highway 50 in Meyers, follow Highway 89 south for 4.3 miles. There will be a turnout on the east (left) side of the road.

Although the meadow is small and surrounded by trees, you can see it on the east side of the highway and adjacent to the parking area. This meadow is a good place to experience ski touring for the first time.

Entering Big Meadow   by Lee Griffith

MAP 31
PAGE 197

Big Meadow **74**

Difficulty	2
Length	1 mile round trip
Elevation	7300/+200,−200
Navigation	Map
Time	Few hours
Season	December through April
USGS topo	7.5′ series, Echo Lake, Freel Peak
Start	From Highway 50 in Meyers, follow Highway 89 south for exactly 5.0 miles. There will be a turnout on the north (left) side of the road.

Although the route itself to Big Meadow is not particularly interesting, the meadow and the surrounding area are a pleasant destination and interesting to explore. Big Meadow is also a landmark on the Scotts Lake tour (no. 75) and the Round Lake and Dardanelles Lake tour (no. 76).

Mileage Log

The tour begins on Highway 89 directly opposite the parking turnout and 50 yards east (uphill) from where Big Meadow Creek crosses the highway.

0.0 – 0.5 +200 **(1)** Ski south along the east (left) side of Big Meadow Creek for 0.5 mile until you reach **Big Meadow (2)**. Stay far enough to the left of the creek to avoid the brush. This route is relatively steep and you will likely find it heavily worn.

Blindly following the author on a scouting trip

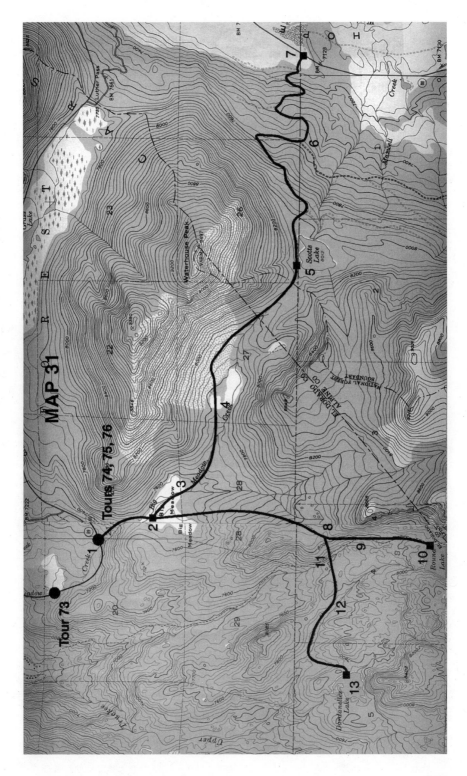

MAP 31

Tours 74, 75, 76

Tour 73

Difficulty	3
Length	5 miles round trip or
	5 miles one-way to Hope Valley
Elevation	7300/+800,–800 round trip or
	7300/+750/–950 one-way to Hope Valley
Navigation	Road and map
Time	Half day
Season	December through April for round trip or
	mid-December through mid-April for one-way to Hope Valley
USGS topo	7.5' series, Echo Lake, Freel Peak
Start	From Highway 50 in Meyers, follow Highway 89 south for exactly 5.0 miles. There will be a turnout on the north (left) side of the road.
End	You can return to the starting point or end the tour on Highway 88 in Hope Valley. The ending point on Highway 88 is 1.5 miles southwest of the junction of Highways 88 and 89 (Picketts Junction). There is an old gate on the west side of the road.

This tour gives you the feeling of seclusion as you navigate through woods. It is a good choice for strong advancing beginner skiers who want to get away from the very easy-to-follow routes of most beginner tours. By making this tour a one-way trip to Hope Valley, you also have a wonderful downhill run, with lots of room to maneuver, from Scotts Lake to the valley.

Mileage Log

The tour begins on Highway 89 directly opposite the parking turnout and 50 yards east (uphill) from where Big Meadow Creek crosses the highway.

0.0 – 0.5   +200 **(1)** Ski south along the east (left) side of Big Meadow Creek for 0.5 mile until you reach **Big Meadow (2)**. Stay far enough to the left of the creek to avoid the brush. This section is relatively steep and you will likely find it heavily worn.

0.5 – 0.7   +0 **(2)** Ski southeast (left) through the meadow for 0.2 mile until you reach the location where **Big Meadow Creek enters the meadow (3)**.

0.7 – 1.4   +300 **(3)** Enter the woods and ski along the creek for 0.7 mile until you reach another **meadow (4)**.

   Locate the road on the far north (left) side of the meadow.

1.4 – 2.7 +250,–50 **(4)** Ski east and then southeast on the road for a total of 1.3 miles until you reach **Scotts Lake (5)**. To the north of the lake is Waterhouse Peak, to the east is Hope Valley, and the horizon to the east is dominated by Pickett and Hawkins peaks.

To continue to Hope Valley

2.7 – 4.1 –400 **(5)** Ski east on the road, which passes on the north side of Scotts Lake, for 1.4 mile until you reach a **road junction (6)**. The road becomes steeper as you descend, and you may prefer to leave the road and pick your own path to the east; this way you will have more room to maneuver. Feel free to zig-zag down through the fairly open woods where the telemarking terrain is excellent.

4.1 – 5.1 –500 **(6)** If you encounter the road junction, follow the fork that heads east (left) for 1.0 mile until you reach **Highway 88 (7)**. If you have already left the road, continue to descend east until you reach the highway.

Lake Tahoe attracts the photographer's eye   by Mark Grimes

76 Round Lake and Dardanelles Lake

MAP 31
PAGE 197

Difficulty	4
Length	5 miles round trip to Round Lake or
	6 miles round trip to Dardanelle Lake
Elevation	7300/+1050,−1050 to Round Lake or
	7300/+1350,−1350 to Dardanelles Lake
Navigation	Map and compass
Time	Full day
Season	Mid-December through mid-April
USGS topo	7.5' series, Echo Lake, Freel Peak, Caples Lake
Start	From Highway 50 in Meyers, follow Highway 89 south for exactly 5.0 miles. There will be a turnout on the north (left) side of the road.

After leaving Big Meadow behind, it is unlikely that you will meet other skiers on this tour to Round Lake or Dardanelles Lake. The need for navigation by map and compass weeds out all but the most adventuresome skiers.

Both Round Lake and Dardanelles Lake are located in the Upper Truckee River drainage. Of the two lakes, Round Lake is easier to find. Dardanelles Lake is more difficult to find because it is situated among trees in a rugged area.

Mileage Log

The tour begins on Highway 89 directly opposite the parking turnout and 50 yards east (uphill) from where Big Meadow Creek crosses the highway.

0.0 – 0.5   +200 **(1)** Ski south along the east (left) side of Big Meadow Creek for 0.5 mile until you reach **Big Meadow (2)**. Stay far enough to the left of the creek to avoid the brush. This section is relatively steep and you will likely find it heavily worn.

0.5– 1.7   +600 **(2)** Ski south across the meadow and then climb gradually south for a total of 1.2 miles until you reach a **saddle (8)**. As you climb, you parallel a creek to the east (left) and traverse a ridge to the west (right). When you are 0.8 mile south of Big Meadow (there is no landmark), veer slightly west (right) for the remaining 0.4 mile to the saddle. To the west of the saddle is the Upper Truckee River drainage.

To Round Lake

1.7 – 2.0   −150 **(8)** Descend the west side of the saddle by traversing to the south for 0.3 mile until you reach more **level terrain (9)**.

2.0 – 2.6   +100 **(9)** Ski south and parallel to the steep cliffs, and pass below a prominent rock outcropping, for a total of 0.6 mile until you reach **Round Lake (10)**.

To Dardanelles Lake

1.7 – 1.9   –300 **(8)** Descend directly down the west side of the saddle for 0.2 mile until the terrain levels and you reach a **creek (11)**. If necessary, ski up stream to cross the creek.

1.9 – 2.2   –50 **(11)** Ski west for 0.3 mile, at first through an open area and then across a frozen pond, and finally down to another **creek (12)**.

2.2 – 3.0   +100,–100 **(12)** Descend along the northeast (right) side of the creek for 0.5 mile, cross the creek and climb south for 0.3 mile to **Dardanelles Lake (13)**. You will find the skiing on its southwest side much more difficult if you are forced to cross the creek upstream of the described location.

Refueling stop

77 Grass Lake

Difficulty	1
Length	Short
Elevation	7700/Nil
Navigation	Adjacent to plowed road
Time	Short
Season	December through April
USGS topo	7.5' series, Freel Peak
Start	Highway 89, anywhere from Luther Pass west for 1.5 miles.

Grass Lake and the meadow surrounding it form a one and one-half-mile long flat area on the south side of Highway 89. Close to South Lake Tahoe, this area is excellent for practicing ski touring techniques. Beginners can experience easy downhill runs on the slopes to the south. On the west end of the meadow, an old road which enters the trees can be followed for a short distance. Be aware that it may not be safe to ski on the lake.

Willow Creek

Difficulty	4
Length	6 miles one-way
Elevation	7700/+1100,−2250
Navigation	Map and compass
Time	Full day
Season	Late December through early April
USGS topo	7.5′ series, Freel Peak, Echo Lake
Start	From Highway 50 in Meyers follow Highway 89 south for 6.8 miles to the first turnout, which borders a meadow and Grass Lake, on the south (right) side of the road. The tour begins on the north side of the road across from the turnout.
End	Tahoe Paradise residential area near Meyers. From Highway 50, follow Apache Avenue into the residential area and find a parking place; Lost Lane is a good location. Dense woods near the end of the tour make it difficult to end it at a specific point; carry a local map of the Meyers area on the tour so that you can find your car.

The beauty of this route is that long after the snow has thawed and consolidated in other areas, this route normally still offers powder snow conditions in the upper reaches of Saxon Creek. Coincidentally, this is the location of the downhill run from Tucker Flat.

This tour also challenges advanced skiers — the terrain is steep, the navigation is critical, and the skiing in the dense woods is difficult.

Mileage Log

0.0 – 0.3   +100 **(4)** Ski northwest for 0.3 mile until you reach a **creek (5)**.

0.3 – 1.7   +1000 **(5)** Climb northeast and parallel to the creek at a steep angle for 1.4 miles until you reach the **saddle (6)** between Peaks 9426 and 9078. Only attempt this ascent when there is absolutely no avalanche danger. Tucker Flat is just to the northeast of the saddle.

1.7 – 3.2   −1200 **(6)** Descend northwest, paralleling but staying above the summer trail and Saxon Creek, for 1.5 miles until you reach an **elevation of 7600 feet (7)**. If you do not have an altimeter, you will have to estimate the correct elevation by carefully comparing the terrain with the topo. The descent in this section is steep, but hopefully covered with powder snow.

78

3.2 – 4.3 −50 **(7)** Turn away from Saxon Creek and the summer trail, and traverse northwest below Peak 8316 and maintain your elevation for 1.1 miles until you reach a more level area on a **ridge (8)**.

4.3 – 5.7 −1000 **(8)** Traverse north for 0.5 mile and then descend northwest for 0.9 mile until you reach the **ending point (9)** at the Tahoe Paradise residential area. Be aware that if you drop down too early you end up in an undergrowth where it is impossible to ski.

Remains of igloo

Difficulty	4
Length	8 miles round trip
Elevation	7700/+1850,–1850
Navigation	Map and compass
Time	Full day
Season	Late December through mid-April
USGS topo	7.5′ series, Freel Peak
Start	From Highway 50 in Meyers follow Highway 89 south for 6.8 miles to the first turnout, which borders a meadow and Grass Lake, on the south (right) side of the road. The tour begins on the north side of the road across from the turnout.

Like the prow of a ship, Thompson Peak stands with an unobstructed view of more than you can imagine. Near, of course, is Hope Valley, but peak after peak to the south are in plain sight. Most obvious are Pickett Peak and Hawkins Peak along with those of the Carson Pass area.

The climb is very steep at first and the route very confined. Therefore, you should pick a time for this tour when you know the snow will be good on the return descent. As an alternative you can end this trip in Hope Valley as described in the Grass Lake to Hope Valley via Thompson Peak tour (no. 80).

Mileage Log

0.0 – 0.3   +100 **(4)** Ski northwest for 0.3 mile until you reach a **creek (5)**.

0.3 – 1.7   +1000 **(5)** Climb northeast and parallel to the creek at a steep angle for 1.4 miles until you reach the **saddle (6)** between Peaks 9426 and 9078. Only attempt this ascent when there is absolutely no avalanche danger.

1.7 – 2.3   +400 **(6)** Ski east on a broad ridge and as you approach the head of the creek that lies to the north leave the ridge and continue east for a total of 0.6 mile until you reach the **west end of Freel Meadows (10)**.

2.3 – 2.8   +0 **(10)** Ski southeast for 0.5 mile to the **southeast end of Freel Meadows (11)**. There is a small section of trees that divide the meadow into two.

2.8 – 3.1   –100 **(11)** Descend to the southeast for 0.3 mile until you reach a small **drainage (12)**.

3.1 – 3.8   +250 **(12)** Ski south, climbing out of the drainage, for 0.7 mile until you reach the **summit of Thompson Peak (13)**.

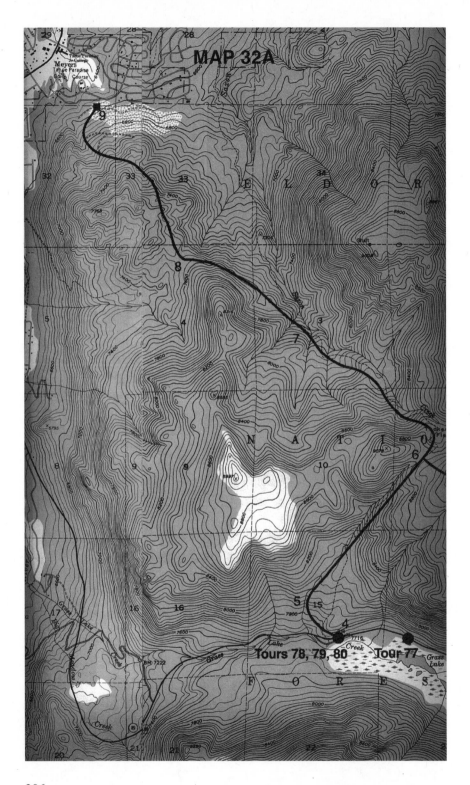

MAP 32A

Tours 78, 79, 80   Tour 77

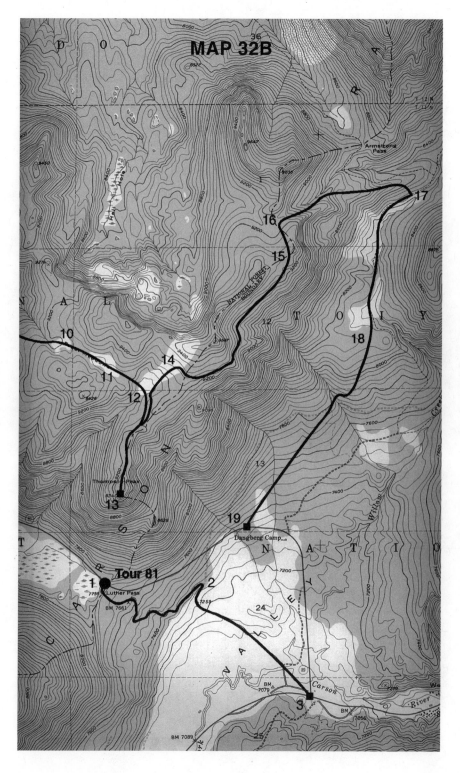

MAP 32B

Tour 81

207

80 Grass Lake to Hope Valley via Thompson Peak

MAP 32A-32B
PAGE 206-207

Difficulty	4
Length	10 miles one-way
Elevation	7700/+2000,–2300
Navigation	Map and compass
Time	Full day
Season	Late December through early April
USGS topo	7.5′ series, Freel Peak
Start	From Highway 50 in Meyers follow Highway 89 south for 6.8 miles to the first turnout, which borders a meadow and Grass Lake, on the south (right) side of the road. The tour begins on the north side of the road across from the turnout.
End	Highway 89, 1.0 mile east of Luther Pass and 1.8 miles north of Picketts Junction (junction of Highways 88 and 89). There is a turnout on the south side of the highway.

This is truly one of the best tours in the South Lake Tahoe area. It transforms the tour to Thompson Peak (no. 79) into a one-way journey that anyone who enjoys exploring will love. A circuitous route and varied terrain keep you anticipating what is ahead. Best of all, on this tour you will feel very much alone.

Mileage Log

0.0 – 3.8 +1750,–100 **(4)** Follow the Thompson Peak tour (no. 79) for 3.8 miles until you reach the **summit of Thompson Peak (13)**.

3.8 – 4.8 +100,–150 **(13)** Ski north and then northeast for a total of 1.0 mile until you reach the **mid-point in an open slope (14)** to the southwest of Peak 9638.

4.8 – 6.1 +150,–150 **(14)** Leave the open area to the east (right) and traverse northeast on a bench for a total of 1.3 miles until you reach **flat terrain (15)** at the northeast end of a ridge.

6.1 – 6.4 –100 **(15)** Descend north for 0.3 mile until you reach a **saddle (16)**.

6.4 – 7.5 –950 **(16)** Descend a drainage northeast, work your way onto the small ridge that heads east, and finally drop southeast off the the ridge for a total of 1.1 miles until you reach **Willow Creek (17)**.

7.5 – 8.6 –100 **(17)** Ski south along Willow Creek for 1.1 miles until you reach a relative **flat, open area (18)**.

8.6 – 10.3 –750 **(18)** Ski southwest, picking up a road somewhere along the way, for 1.7 miles until you reach the **ending point (19)**.

Luther Pass to Hope Valley **81**

Difficulty	3
Length	3 miles one-way
Elevation	7750/–700
Navigation	Road
Time	Few hours
Season	Mid-December through mid-April
USGS topo	7.5' series, Freel Peak
Start	Luther Pass on Highway 89.
End	Picketts Junction (intersection of Highways 88 and 89) in Hope Valley.

This is a 100-percent downhill run from Luther Pass to Hope Valley. It takes so little time to complete this tour that you will surely want to extend the day by skiing at nearby Grass Lake (no. 77).

Consider parking at the west end of Grass Lake and skiing the complete length of the Grass Lake area; that will add more than a mile. If you do so, remember that there is a second meadow to the east of the large meadow and separated by trees. This tour starts at the east end of that second meadow.

Mileage Log

Locate the snow-covered road and the start of the tour at Luther Pass. A snowplow turn-around is located here so you will probably have to start skiing a little to the west. Regardless, the road is located in the trees at the east end of the small meadow.

0.0 – 1.2   –450 **(1)** Descend on the road for 1.2 miles until you reach a **180-degree right turn (2)**.

1.2 – 2.5   –250 **(2)** Continue on the road and when you enter the open area of Hope Valley continue southeast for a total of 1.3 miles until you reach **Picketts Junction (3)**.

Approaching microwave tower on Huckleberry Ridge

Echo Summit

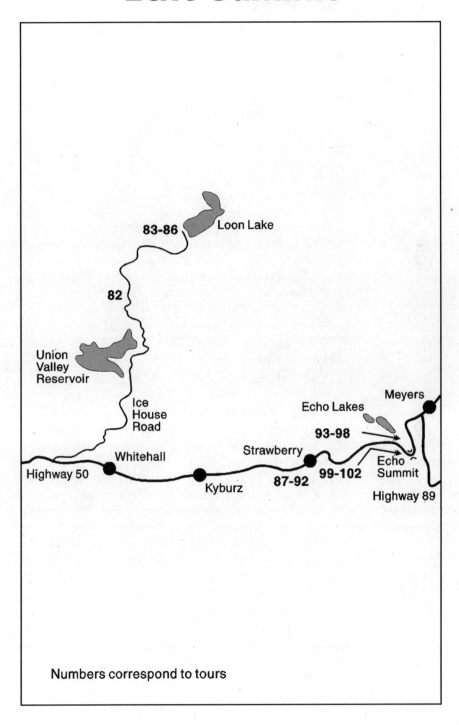

Loon Lake

83-86

82

Union
Valley
Reservoir

Ice
House
Road

Echo Lakes

Meyers

93-98

Whitehall

Strawberry

Highway 50

Kyburz

87-92

99-102

Echo
Summit

Highway 89

Numbers correspond to tours

Difficulty	3
Length	5 miles round trip via short route, 9 miles round trip via long route, or 8 miles round trip via the loop
Elevation	5650/+1050,–1050 via short route, 5400/+1300,–1300 via long route, or 5650/+1300,–1300 via the loop
Navigation	Road and map
Time	Half day to most of a day
Season	January through March
USGS topo	7.5' series, Robbs Peak
Start	From Highway 50 turn north onto Ice House Road and drive for 21 miles until you reach a saddle. Continue for 0.8 mile until you reach a snow-covered road on the west (left) side of Ice House Road which marks the starting point of the "short route." The "long route" starts 1.2 miles ahead on the west (left) side of Ice House Road at the snow-covered road that heads to Uncle Toms Cabin. The road to Uncle Toms Cabin is located 100 yards before the turnoff to South Fork Campground.

The presence of a fire lookout atop Robbs Peak attests to a commanding view. As you enjoy a leisurely lunch at the summit, look east to the impressive Crystal Range. After lunch, you can practice your telemark turns on the gradual slopes near the summit.

Although the tour to Robbs Peak can be completed easily in one day, consider spending a night at the top. In 1986, 70 volunteers pitched in to convert the abandoned lookout's facilities into a usable hut. The sleeping accommodations include a bunkhouse with a picture window that faces the Crystal Range. But the real highlight is the social area in the lookout; the windows on all sides make it a wonderful place to cook, eat, read, play games or just admire a magnificent sunrise or sunset as the flames flicker in the stove. For information and reservations contact:

Eldorado National Forest Information Center
3070 Camino Heights Drive
Camino, CA 95709
(916) 644-6048

Mileage Log

Short Route

0.0 – 0.1   +100 **(1)** Climb west through a clearing toward the trees for 0.1 mile until you reach the **road (2)** running north-south and parallel to the trees.

0.1 – 1.6   +600 **(2)** Ski south on the road for 1.5 miles until you reach a distinct **saddle (3)** located to the south of Robbs Peak.

1.6 – 2.5   +350 **(3)** Ski north on the road for 0.9 mile until you reach the lookout atop **Robbs Peak (4)**. The road traverses along the east side of the south ridge of Robbs Peak and leads to the open slopes of the summit.

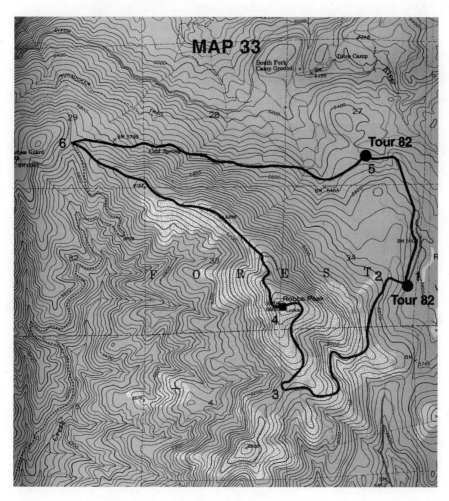

82

Long Route

0.0 – 2.2   +500 **(5)** Climb very gradually to the west for 2.2 miles on the snow-covered road that heads to Uncle Toms Cabin until you reach a **saddle (6)**.

> *At the saddle, locate the junction between the road you are on and an obvious road that gradually descends to the south. At this road junction, there is also an obscure road that climbs southeast along a ridge. This is the road on which the tour continues.*

2.2 – 4.3   +800 **(6)** Climb southeast on the obscure road and ridge for 2.1 miles until you reach the **summit of Robbs Peak (4)**.

Loop tour

The ideal way to visit Robbs Peak is to make a loop by ascending via the short route and descending via the long route. When you have returned to the starting point of the long route, ski south on the west side of and parallel to Ice House Road for 1.1 miles and 250 feet of elevation gain until you reach the starting point of the short route. You can follow an abandoned road for part of this distance.

View from Robbs Peak   by Dick Simpson

MAP 34
PAGE 216

Berts Lake and Peak 6836

83

Difficulty	3
Length	2 miles round trip
Elevation	6400/+450,−450
Navigation	Marked trail and map
Time	Few hours
Season	Late December through early April
USGS topo	7.5' series, Loon Lake
Start	Near Loon Lake on Ice House Road. From Highway 50 turn north onto Ice House Road. Drive 24 miles to the intersection where you must turn right to stay on Ice House Road. Turn right and continue for 5.4 miles until you reach the powerhouse building on the east (right) side of the road. Continue for another 100 yards to a parking area on the west (left) side of the road.

This very short tour to Berts Lake and Peak 6836 is an excellent choice for skiers who want to experience a tour of intermediate difficulty for the first time. The views from the lake and the peak make this excursion well worth the effort.

Mileage Log

At the parking area, locate the SMUD rain gauge and the markers which lead south. Follow the markers as best you can, but don't be surprised if you lose them.

0.0 – 0.3   +200 **(1)** Climb south up the nose of a ridge for 0.3 mile until you reach the **level section of the ridge (2)** to the north of Peak 6836.

0.3 – 1.0   +100 **(2)** Ski southeast along the east side of Peak 6836 and then loop west for a total of 0.7 mile until you reach a saddle and **Berts Lake (3)**.

1.0 – 1.1   +150 **(3)** Climb northeast for 0.1 mile until you reach the **summit of Peak 6836 (4)**.

From Berts Lake, you can return to the starting point by retracing your route or by descending to the west until you intersect the Chipmunk Bluff tour (no. 84) which you can follow back to the starting point.

215

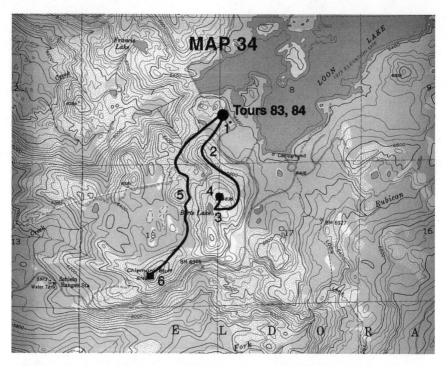

Enjoying the rewards of the climb

MAP 34
PAGE 216

Chipmunk Bluff **84**

Difficulty	2
Length	3 miles round trip
Elevation	6400/+350,−350
Navigation	Road
Time	Half day
Season	Late December through early April
USGS topo	7.5′ series, Loon Lake
Start	Near Loon Lake on Ice House Road. From Highway 50 turn north onto Ice House Road. Drive 24 miles to the intersection where you must turn right to stay on Ice House Road. Turn right and continue for 5.4 miles until you reach the powerhouse building on the east (right) side of the road. Continue for another 100 yards to a parking area on the west (left) side of the road.

This pleasant tour on a road is ideal for skiers seeking a short, easy tour. From the vicinity of Chipmunk Bluff there are good views to enjoy while partaking of lunch. Be aware that the last 75 vertical feet to the summit of Chipmunk Bluff are not skiable and are dangerous to climb due to the precipitous angle and the presence of cornices at the top.

Mileage Log

0.0 – 0.7   +150 **(1)** Ski southwest on the snow-covered road for 0.5 mile until you reach power lines and then continue for 0.2 mile until you reach a **saddle (5)**.

0.7 – 1.4   +150,−50 **(5)** Descend south and then ascend southwest for a total of 0.7 mile until you reach the base of the **very steep section that leads to the summit of Chipmunk Bluff (6)**.

MAP 35
PAGE 219

85 South Shore of Loon Lake

Difficulty	1 – 2
Length	Up to 7 miles round trip
Elevation	6400/Nil
Navigation	Adjacent to plowed road and map
Time	Up to most of a day
Season	Late December through early April
USGS topo	7.5′ series, Loon Lake, Wentworth Springs
Start	End of plowed road at Loon Lake. From Highway 50 turn north onto Ice House Road. Drive 24 miles to the intersection where you must turn right to stay on Ice House Road. Turn right and continue for 5.4 miles until you reach the powerhouse building on the east (right) side of the road. Continue for 100 yards until you pass a parking area on the west (left) side of the road and then another 100 yards to the end of the plowed road.

Although this tour is not difficult, skiers of all abilities can enjoy the unusual beauty of Loon Lake. The stark setting created by the vast lake basin, surrounding granite peaks, and sparse greenery will make you feel like you are on the moon.

On this tour along the south shore of Loon Lake you will encounter fewer snowmobiles than on the tour along the north shore. Directions for connecting the south and north shore tours are also described in this tour.

Mileage Log

0.0 – 0.4   +0 **(1)** Ski down to the edge of and then south along the lake for 0.4 mile until you reach a **powerhouse building (2)** (not the one by the road) just before reaching the south end of the lake. Due to fluctuating water levels, the ice on Loon Lake is unstable and dangerous; stay off the lake.

0.4 – 2.4   +0 **(2)** Ski up and around the powerhouse building, around the south end of the lake, and then northeast for a total of 2.0 miles until you reach the **building at Deer Crossing (3)**. The terrain is filled with very gradual slopes and small rock outcroppings around which to weave.

2.4 – 3.5   +0 **(3)** Ski northeast along Loon Lake and then along Pleasant Lake for a total of 1.1 miles until you reach a **tunnel (4)** in the cliff. This tunnel connects Buck Island Lake Reservoir with Pleasant Lake and marks the farthest point of this tour.

*Connecting the South Shore of Loon Lake tour
with the North Shore of Loon Lake tour (no. 86)*

You can continue to the North Shore of Loon Lake tour by skiing around the
north end of Pleasant Lake where you can expect to negotiate many small
obstacles, the most difficult of which is the creek formed by water exiting the
tunnel. One mile before reaching the northern dam of Loon Lake (the destination of the North Shore of Loon Lake tour) expect to cross or ski around
several small ridges and gullies. The distance of the loop around Loon and
Pleasant lakes is 7.0 miles.

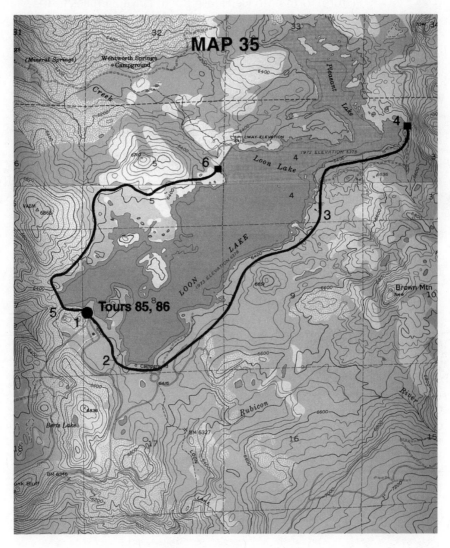

Difficulty	1
Length	Up to 4 miles round trip
Elevation	6400/Nil
Navigation	Road
Time	Up to half day
Season	Late December through early April
USGS topo	7.5′ series, Loon Lake, Wentworth Springs
Start	End of plowed road at Loon Lake. From Highway 50 turn north onto Ice House Road. Drive 24 miles to the intersection where you must turn right to stay on Ice House Road. Turn right and continue for 5.4 miles until you reach the powerhouse building on the east (right) side of the road. Continue for 100 yards until you pass a parking area on the west (left) side of the road and then another 100 yards to the end of the plowed road.

The tour along the north shore of Loon Lake is the easiest tour in this area and offers beginners an opportunity to experience skiing in this stark, yet beautiful, basin.

If you prefer to avoid the road, but want an easy tour, consider the South Shore of Loon Lake tour (no. 85). Its description also provides information about circumnavigating Loon and Pleasant lakes.

Mileage Log

0.0 – 0.1   +0 **(1)** Ski northwest on the snow-covered road for 0.1 mile until you reach the **southern dam (5)**.

0.1 – 2.0   +0 **(5)** Ski across the dam and then continue on the road for 1.9 miles until you reach the **northern dam (6)** which is the destination of this tour.

Strawberry Canyon Road 87

Difficulty	2 – 3
Length	Up to 9 miles round trip
Elevation	5650/+1250,–1250
Navigation	Road
Time	Up to full day
Season	Late December through early April
USGS topo	7.5′ series, Pyramid Peak, Echo Lake
Start	42-Mile Recreation Site on Highway 50, 0.5 mile southwest of Strawberry.

One good reason for choosing to ski in the 42-Mile Recreation Site area is its proximity to Sacramento and the Bay Area. Of all the tours beginning at the site trailhead, Strawberry Canyon Road, which parallels the north side of Strawberry Creek, is least used.

This tour has no particular destination and you can tailor the length to your desires. The track you make while climbing very gradually up the road makes for an excellent glide on your return.

Mileage Log

0.0 – 0.6 +150 **(1)** Cross the bridge to the southeast side of the South Fork of the American River, immediately turn south (right) toward Strawberry Creek Tract, and ski on the road for 0.6 mile until you reach the **junction (2)** of Strawberry Canyon and Cody Summit roads. In this section, stay on the obvious main road and ignore the small roads which lead into the cabin areas.

0.6 – 0.8 +50 **(2)** Turn north (left) onto Strawberry Canyon Road and ski for 0.2 mile until you reach the location where the **main road turns (3)** southeast (right) and you pass a small road on your left.

0.8 – 2.5 +350 **(3)** Ski southeast on the main road for 1.7 miles until you reach an impressive, awe-inspiring **avalanche chute (4)** created in the winter of 1983. That season's record snowfall left a huge snowpack on this steep slope. When warm weather followed, the melted snow saturated the decomposed granite to form a quicksand-like mass. Even the dense stand of large, mature trees could not hold back its weight.

2.5 – 3.9 +250 **(4)** Ski southeast on the road for 1.4 miles until you reach a **gate (5)**.

3.9 – 4.6 +200,–250 **(5)** Ski south on the road for 0.7 mile until you reach **Strawberry Creek (6)**. You can cross the creek and follow an obscure road still farther up Strawberry Canyon.

221

Difficulty	3
Length	5 miles round trip
Elevation	5650/+1100,–1100
Navigation	Road and marked trail
Time	Half day
Season	Late December through early April
USGS topo	7.5′ series, Pyramid Peak
Start	42-Mile Recreation Site on Highway 50, 0.5 mile southwest of Strawberry.

The highlight of this tour is having lunch on the ridge above Strawberry Canyon. Along the route you will find an assortment of wide and narrow roads, and mild and steep slopes.

Mileage Log

0.0 – 0.6 +150 **(1)** Cross the bridge to the southeast side of the South Fork of the American River, immediately turn south (right) toward Strawberry Creek Tract, and ski on the road for 0.6 mile until you reach the **junction (2)** of Strawberry Canyon and Cody Summit roads. In this section, stay on the obvious main road and ignore the small roads which lead into the cabin areas.

0.6 – 0.8 +0 **(2)** Continue on the fork to the southeast (right) for 0.2 mile until you reach the bridge at **Strawberry Creek (7)**.

0.8 – 0.9 +50 **(7)** Immediately after crossing the creek, turn southeast (left) at a road junction, and ski parallel to the creek for 0.1 mile until you reach a **road junction (8)**. You will return to this point on the road from the west (right).

0.9 – 1.4 +150 **(8)** Continue to ski southeast (straight) on the road for 0.5 mile until you reach a **road junction (9)**. Past this junction, the route climbs at a much steeper angle.

1.4 – 2.0 +300 **(9)** Take the south (right) fork and ski on the road for 0.6 mile until you reach a **180-degree right turn (10)**.

2.0 – 2.3 +200 **(10)** Ski on the road for 0.3 mile until you reach a 180-degree left turn and ski 100 yards farther until you reach a **marker (11)** which indicates where the route leaves the main road.

2.3 – 2.8 +250 **(11)** Follow the marked trail, which follows an obscure road, and climb southwest for 0.5 mile to the **ridge top (12)**. If you still want to climb after reaching the ridge top, you can explore the ridge before resuming the tour.

2.8 – 2.9 –150 **(12)** Descend from the ridge to the southwest for 0.1 mile until you reach a jeep **road (13)**.

2.9 – 3.3 –300 **(13)** Follow the jeep road as it gradually turns north (right) for 0.4 mile until you reach a clearing to the northwest; leave the road and descend the clearing for 75 yards until you intersect another **jeep road (14)** and the Cody Creek Loop (no. 90). You have skied too far on the first jeep road if it begins to turn east (right).

3.3 – 3.7 –200 **(14)** Continue north on the merged trails (an obscure road) for 0.4 mile until you reach a small **ridge (15)**.

3.7 – 4.0 –250 **(15)** Ski northeast on the jeep trail for 0.1 mile and then on a regular road for 0.2 mile until you reach the **road junction (8)** you encountered earlier in the tour.

4.0 – 4.9 –200 **(8)** Turn northwest (left) and retrace your tracks for 0.9 mile until you reach the **starting point (1)**.

Sharing the summit with friends

Pyramid Peak from Packsaddle Pass road

Station Creek Trail **89**

Difficulty	2
Length	5 miles round trip
Elevation	5650/+450,−450
Navigation	Road and marked trail
Time	Half day
Season	Late December through early April
USGS topo	7.5′ series, Pyramid Peak
Start	42-Mile Recreation Site on Highway 50, 0.5 mile southwest of Strawberry.

This tour takes you on easy-to-follow and gradually sloping roads to a beautiful view of the South Fork of the American River Canyon, the sheer rock face of Lovers Leap, and Ralston Peak.

Mileage Log

0.0 – 0.6 +150 **(1)** Cross the bridge to the southeast side of the South Fork of the American River, immediately turn south (right) toward Strawberry Creek Tract, and ski on the road for 0.6 mile until you reach the **junction (2)** of Strawberry Canyon and Cody Summit roads. In this section, stay on the obvious main road and ignore the small roads which lead into the cabin areas.

0.6 – 0.8 +0 **(2)** Continue on the fork to the southeast (right) for 0.2 mile until you reach the bridge at **Strawberry Creek (7)**.

0.8 – 1.6 +150 **(7)** Immediately after crossing the creek, pass a lesser road on your left and continue skiing west (straight) for 0.8 mile until you reach a road **junction (16)**.

1.6 – 2.5 −150 **(16)** Take the northwest (right) fork and descend for 0.9 mile until you reach an **excellent view (17)** to the northeast.

2.5 – 2.7 +0 **(17)** Ski west on the road for 0.2 mile until you reach an even **better view (18)**. You can see Lovers Leap up the canyon. Beyond here the road(s) continue, however, there is no particularly good destination.

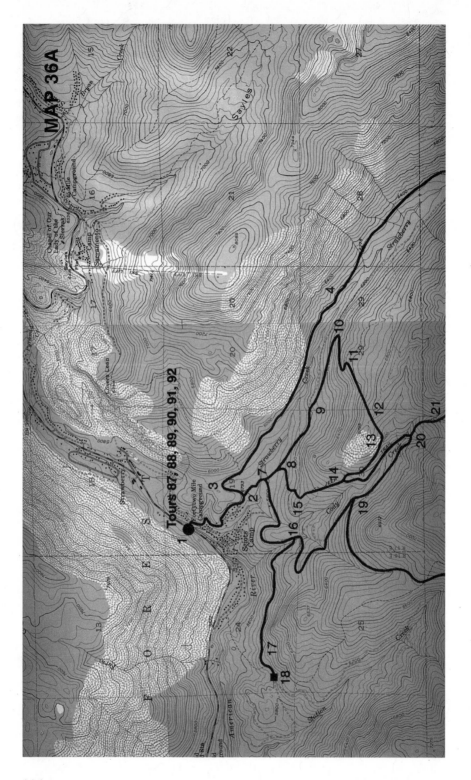

MAP 36A

Tours 87, 88, 89, 90, 91, 92

226

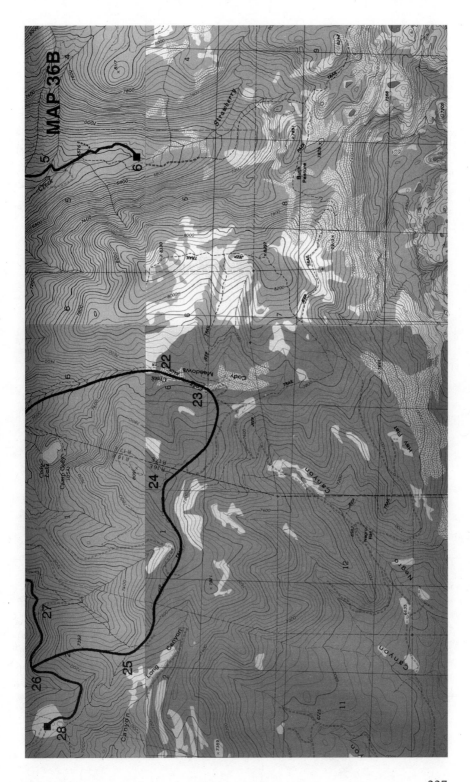

MAP 36B

Difficulty	3
Length	5 miles round trip
Elevation	5650/+900,−900
Navigation	Road and marked trail
Time	Half day
Season	Late December through early April
USGS topo	7.5′ series, Pyramid Peak
Start	42-Mile Recreation Site on Highway 50, 0.5 mile southwest of Strawberry.

This tour follows a road that climbs very gradually until it heads up Cody Creek where the gradient steepens slightly as the canyon closes in. If you are just progressing into intermediate touring, note that this loop is slightly easier than the nearby Strawberry Ridge Loop tour (no. 88).

Mileage Log

0.0 – 0.6 +150 **(1)** Cross the bridge to the southeast side of the South Fork of the American River, immediately turn south (right) toward Strawberry Creek Tract, and ski on the road for 0.6 mile until you reach the **junction (2)** of Strawberry Canyon and Cody Summit roads. In this section, stay on the obvious main road and ignore the small roads which lead into the cabin areas.

0.6 – 0.8 +0 **(2)** Continue on the fork to the southeast (right) for 0.2 mile until you reach the bridge at **Strawberry Creek (7)**.

0.8 – 1.6 +150 **(7)** Immediately after crossing the creek, pass a lesser road on your left and continue skiing west (straight) for 0.8 mile until you reach a **road junction (16)**. The northwest (right) fork is part of the Station Creek Trail (no. 89).

1.6 – 2.6 +400 **(16)** Take the south (left) fork and almost immediately pass a road on your left, continue west (right) for 0.3 mile until you make a 180-degree left turn, and ski southeast for 0.7 mile until you reach a **road junction (19)**. This junction may look like a turn to the right, not a junction. The main fork to the west (right) leads to Packsaddle Pass (no. 92). Note that between the 180-degree turn and the desired road junction you will pass a road on your right that ascends at a steep angle.

2.6 – 3.2 +200 **(19)** Continue on the lesser road, marked with blue diamonds, to the southeast (straight) for 0.6 mile until you reach **Cody Creek (20)**.

After crossing Cody Creek, locate the marked jeep trail that turns back 180 degrees to the northwest. If you encounter a sign indicating "No Cross Country Trail System Beyond This Point," you have past the jeep trail.

3.2 – 3.8 –250 **(20)** Ski northwest on the jeep road for 0.6 mile until you reach the **junction (14)** (there is no landmark here) with the Strawberry Ridge Loop tour (no. 88).

3.8 – 4.2 –200 **(14)** Continue north on the merged trails (an obscure road) for 0.4 mile until you reach a small **ridge (15)**.

4.2 – 4.5 –250 **(15)** Ski northeast on the jeep trail for 0.1 mile and then on a regular road for 0.2 mile until you reach a **road junction (8)**.

4.5 – 4.6 –50 **(8)** Turn northwest (left) and ski 0.1 mile until you reach the bridge across **Strawberry Creek (7)**.

4.6 – 5.4 –150 **(7)** Cross the bridge and retrace your tracks for 0.8 mile until you reach the **starting point (1)**.

Ascending broad ridge on return from Cody Ski Hut

91 Cody Meadow Loop

MAP 36A-36B
PAGE 226-227

Difficulty	5
Length	13 miles round trip
Elevation	5650/+2400,−2400
Navigation	Road, marked trail, map and compass
Time	Very long day
Season	Late December through early April
USGS topo	7.5′ series, Pyramid Peak, Tragedy Spring
Start	42-Mile Recreation Site on Highway 50, 0.5 mile southwest of Strawberry.

Cody Meadow, half-way between Highways 50 and 88, lies in the heart of excellent touring terrain. However, the time necessary to get to and from the meadow leaves little to explore the environs.

A cabin, built by cattle ranchers, is located in the meadow. It was converted to a ski hut, Cody Ski Hut, in the early 1980s by Fred Hartmeyer, a gentle man with the dream of a three-hut system in this area. His efforts, guiding people into the hut most winter weekends, drew attention to this area and its value to Nordic skiers. Now closed to skiers, the hut is unfortunately falling into disrepair.

The loop tour to Cody Meadow is an exercise in navigation unless you have been there before. The difficulty rating of the tour would be a notch less if it were not for the map and compass work required on the return. Unfortunately, from an enjoyment standpoint, retracing your tracks back to the starting point is no substitute for the wonderful ridge skiing on the described return route.

Mileage Log

0.0 – 3.2   +900 **(1)** Follow the Cody Creek Loop tour (no. 90) for 3.2 miles until you reach **Cody Creek (20)**.

3.2 – 3.5   +350 **(20)** Cross the creek, locate a sign that says "No Cross Country Trail System Beyond This Point," ski beyond the sign, turn south on what appears to be a jeep trail, and ascend along Cody Creek for 0.3 mile until you reach the location where the **steepness of the terrain lessens (21)**. This point is at the base of a small ridge.

3.5 – 4.7   +650 **(21)** Continue on the east (left) side of a small ridge and ski south up the wooded Cody Creek drainage for 1.2 miles until you reach the **north end of Cody Meadow (22)**.

4.7 – 5.1   +50 **(22)** Ski south through the meadow for 0.4 mile until you reach a **cabin (23)**; this was Cody Ski Hut. If time permits, climb up a broad ridge east of the cabin until you reach a saddle from which you have views of Elephants Back, Round Top, and the Kirkwood area. It is 1.0 mile and a 550-foot elevation gain to the saddle. However, aside from the views, the descent offers wide open space for many linked turns.

5.1 – 6.0   +450 **(23)** Climb northwest from the cabin on a very broad, moderately wooded ridge for 0.9 mile until you reach the **intersection with another ridge (24)**. This is the high point of the tour.

6.0 – 7.4   –600 **(24)** Ski west and then northwest on a broad ridge for a total of 1.4 miles until you reach the point where the **ridge forks (25)**. The first 0.1 mile of this section is through very dense forest but you come out onto the broad ridge that you continue to follow.

7.4 – 8.1   –450 **(25)** Turn north (right), ski along a broad ridge, and then descend the ridge's west (left) nose for a total of 0.7 mile until you reach a **snow-covered road (26)**. Be aware that if you descend the east (right) nose you will reach a snow-covered road just to the south of road junction 27. In this case you must ski north (left) until you reach the junction and the route described.

8.1 – 8.5   –100 **(26)** Turn east (right) and follow the road for 0.4 mile until you reach a **road junction (27)**.

8.5 – 10.0   –550 **(27)** Take the north (left) fork and follow the road north and east for 1.5 miles until reach another **road junction (19)**. This point is on the route you skied earlier to Cody Creek.

10.0 – 12.6 –700 **(19)** Turn northwest (left) and retrace your tracks for 2.6 miles until you reach the **starting point (1)**.

92 Packsaddle Pass

Difficulty	3
Length	11 miles round trip
Elevation	5650/+1500,–1500
Navigation	Road
Time	Full day
Season	Late December through early April
USGS topo	7.5' series, Pyramid Peak
Start	42-Mile Recreation Site on Highway 50, 0.5 mile southwest of Strawberry.

Packsaddle Pass lies on a broad ridge — so broad that it resembles a wide, open plateau. Here, the terrain is excellent for exploring but the half-day or so you spend climbing leaves little time to wander.

The wonderful view of Pyramid Peak's smooth, tapering profile and of the Crystal Range are the rewards for the long, gradual climb on a wide road that is used regularly by snowmobiles. Expect the views to be obscured by trees until you are within a mile of the pass. Of course it is an easy glide on your return trip.

Mileage Log

0.0 – 2.6 +700 **(1)** Follow the Cody Creek Loop tour (no. 90) for 2.6 miles until you reach the **road junction (19)** where that tour and the Packsaddle Pass tour split.

2.6 – 4.1 +550 **(19)** Turn west (right) and follow the road for 1.5 miles until you reach a **road junction (27)**.

4.1 – 5.3 +250 **(27)** Continue on the fork to the west (right) for 1.2 miles until you reach **Packsaddle Pass (28)**.

MAP 37
PAGE 235

Echo Summit 93

Difficulty	1 – 2
Length	Up to 2 miles round trip
Elevation	Up to 7350/+100,–100
Navigation	Marked trail
Time	Few hours
Season	December through April
USGS topo	7.5' series, Echo Lake
Start	Echo Lake SnoPark. From 1.2 miles west of the Echo Summit Maintenance Station on Highway 50, drive 0.6 mile east towards Berkeley Camp to the SnoPark.

Years ago a Nordic center operating in conjunction with the now defunct alpine ski area at Echo Summit groomed Nordic trails on the north side of Highway 50. In a cooperative effort between the Forest Service and volunteers, in 1994 trails were re-marked in this area of mildly rolling, forested terrain. There are three marked loops located approximately as shown on the map.

Cody Ski Hut   by Lee Griffith

94 Becker Peak

MAP 37
PAGE 235

Difficulty	3
Length	3 miles round trip
Elevation	7350/+1000,−1000
Navigation	Road and map
Time	Few hours
Season	Mid-December through mid-April
USGS topo	7.5′ series, Echo Lake
Start	Echo Lake SnoPark. From 1.2 miles west of the Echo Summit Maintenance Station on Highway 50, drive 0.6 mile east towards Berkeley Camp to the SnoPark.

The Becker Peak tour is the most rewarding short tour in the Echo Summit area. The route along a ridge offers excellent ski touring and magnificent views of Lake Tahoe, Echo Lakes, Talking Mountain, and the mountains to the south. Because this route is so enjoyable, don't feel compelled to reach the summit, the ascent of which can be tricky and dangerous.

Mileage Log

0.0 – 0.4 +100 **(1)** Locate the snow-covered road on the opposite side of the plowed road from the SnoPark and follow it northwest toward Echo Lakes for 0.4 mile until you reach the **location where you must leave the road (2)** to climb onto the ridge of which Becker Peak is a part. There is no landmark where you must leave the road.

0.4 – 0.7 +250 **(2)** Leave the road and climb northwest for 0.3 mile until you reach the **east end of the ridge (3)**.

0.7 – 1.4 +300 **(3)** Ski west along the ridge until you reach a **small high point (4)** which juts up from the ridge. Up to this point, you will find the ridge broad and gently sloped except for one short, narrow section which is passable without much difficulty. Enjoy the fine views, but stay away from the steep northern edges.

Ahead is the crux of the tour. You should be aware of possible avalanche conditions and ice if you choose to proceed beyond this point.

1.4 – 1.7 +350 **(4)** Climb west toward the high point, at an appropriate point (there is no landmark) traverse around Becker Peak's south side until you reach its southwest side, and then climb the last steep but straight forward 250 feet until you reach the **summit of Becker Peak (5)**. The last 50 vertical feet over rocks may be dangerous due to icy conditions.

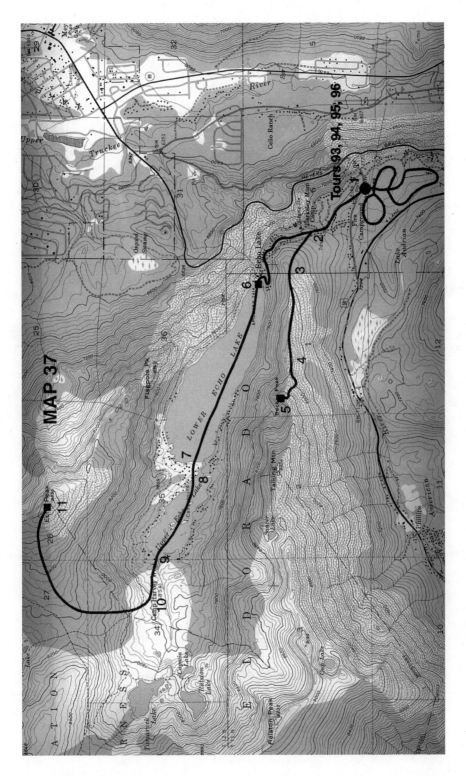

MAP 37

Tours 93, 94, 95, 96

95 Echo Lakes

MAP 37
PAGE 235

Difficulty	2
Length	2 to 6 miles round trip
Elevation	7350/+250,–250
Navigation	Road
Time	Few hours to half day
Season	January through March
USGS topo	7.5′ series, Echo Lake
Start	Echo Lake SnoPark. From 1.2 miles west of the Echo Summit Maintenance Station on Highway 50, drive 0.6 mile east towards Berkeley Camp to the SnoPark.

With lots of room to ski, Echo Lakes is a popular and beautiful destination. The lakes are a perfect place for a leisurely day or night tour; by moonlight the skiing seems effortless over the glowing lakes.

However, Echo Lakes are notorious for windy conditions. When the winds are strong, two people holding a jacket between them, or even better a small tarp, can literally sail across the hard surface at an amazingly high speed. Kite flying can also be great if you have a durable one and unbreakable string.

Echo Lakes are usually solid enough to safely ski on during the months of January, February and March. Regardless of the month, you should always assess the conditions before skiing on the lakes. If Echo Lakes are not safe to ski on, you can ski along the edge where the summer trail skirts them. Unfortunately, the slow and more difficult skiing along the trail is no substitute for the open, hard-packed surface of the lakes.

Please stay away from the many privately owned cabins at Echo Lakes. Also, be aware that overnight camping is not permitted in the lakes basin.

Mileage Log

0.0 – 1.1 +150,–100 **(1)** Locate the snow-covered road on the opposite side of the plowed road from the SnoPark and follow it northwest for 1.1 miles until you reach the **southeast end of Lower Echo Lake (6)**. You can expect a gradual climb followed by a short but steep descent to the lake.

1.1 – 2.5 +0 **(6)** If it is safe, ski northwest across the lower lake for 1.4 miles until you reach its **northwest end (7)**.

2.5 – 2.6 +0 **(7)** Ski northwest for 0.1 mile until you reach the **southeast end of Upper Echo Lake (8)**.

2.6 – 3.2 +0 **(8)** Ski northwest across the upper lake for 0.6 mile until you reach its **northwest end (9)**.

MAP 37
PAGE 235

Echo Peak 96

Difficulty	4
Length	10 miles round trip
Elevation	7350/+1750,−1750
Navigation	Road and map
Time	Full day
Season	January through March
USGS topo	7.5′ series, Echo Lake
Start	Echo Lake SnoPark. From 1.2 miles west of the Echo Summit Maintenance Station on Highway 50, drive 0.6 mile east towards Berkeley Camp to the SnoPark.

The climb to the rocky summit of Echo Peak is a 100 percent perfect tour for skiers desiring to tackle their first ski ascent. Easy access, although more than three miles to the start of the climb, and the easy route-finding will give newcomers to peak bagging a sense of security. Skiers skilled in the art of telemarking can enjoy 1500 feet of linked turns on the descent.

The climbing, through a mixture of open and wooded areas, is steady and the gradient only modestly steep for a peak climb. The view from the summit is a 360-degree panorama — an ideal setting for a well deserved lunch. Directly below the steep cliffs to the north are Angora Lakes and almost at your finger tips are Fallen Leaf Lake and Lake Tahoe. Of course, you will have more than sufficient opportunity to enjoy the Echo Lakes basin and the views to the south.

One word of advice for planning a trip to Echo Peak. Because the entire ascent is on south-facing slopes, new fallen snow quickly turns to mush in afternoon sun. Therefore, unless you make your ascent during or immediately after a storm, it is best to plan this tour for a time when the snow is consolidated.

Mileage Log

0.0 – 3.2 +150,−100 **(1)** Follow the Echo Lakes tour (no. 95) for 3.2 miles until you reach the **northwest end of Upper Echo Lake (9)**.

3.2 – 3.5 +150 **(9)** Ski west for 0.3 mile until the **terrain to the north becomes less steep (10)** (there is no landmark).

3.5 – 5.0 +1350 **(10)** Turn north and steadily climb north and northeast for a total of 1.5 miles until you reach the **summit of Echo Peak (11)**.

97 Desolation Valley

Difficulty	4
Length	12 miles round trip
Elevation	7350/+1450,−1450
Navigation	Road, map and compass
Time	Full day
Season	January through March
USGS topo	7.5' series, Echo Lake, Pyramid Peak
Start	Echo Lake SnoPark. From 1.2 miles west of the Echo Summit Maintenance Station on Highway 50, drive 0.6 mile east towards Berkeley Camp to the SnoPark.

As you make your final descent to Lake Aloha, the heart of Desolation Valley, you are struck by the large, stark valley, the Crystal Range, and the smooth profile of Pyramid Peak. If you are planning a one-day trip to this area, expect to get only a glimpse of its beauty. To fully enjoy the valley's magnificence you must plan a multi-day trip.

The tour to Desolation Valley covers a variety of terrain and is a challenging trip. The first part of this tour is across the very popular Echo Lakes. However, when you leave the lakes behind, you also leave most of the skiers behind. More dramatic is the contrast between Desolation Valley in the winter and in the summer when backpackers flock to this mountain haven.

Mileage Log

0.0 – 3.2 +150,−100 **(1)** Follow the Echo Lakes tour (no. 95) for 3.2 miles until you reach the **northwest end of upper Echo Lake (2)**.

3.2 – 4.8 +900 **(2)** Climb steadily northwest for 1.6 miles until you reach **Haypress Meadows (3)**. In this section you will pass nearby Tamarack and Ralston lakes which are good destinations in their own rights.

4.8 – 5.6 +50,−50 **(3)** Ski northwest for 0.8 mile until you reach the **level area west of Lake Margery (4)**. The best route in this section passes to the west of the lake.

5.6 – 6.0 −200 **(4)** Descend northwest for 0.4 mile until you reach the shore of **Lake Aloha (5)**.

Echo Peak

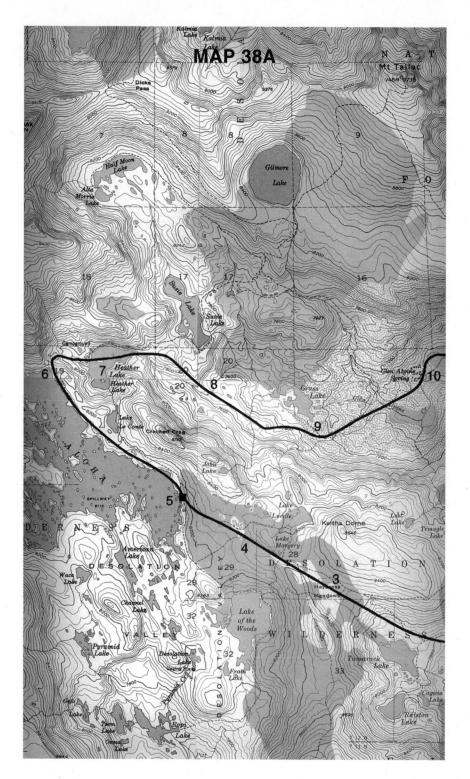

MAP 38A

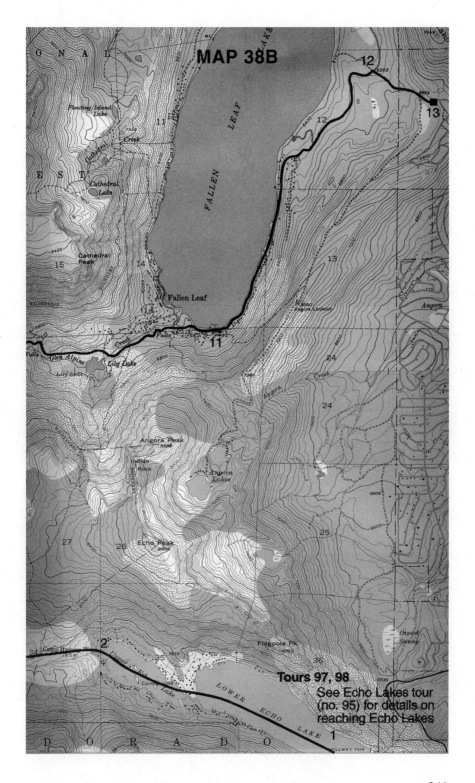

MAP 38B

Tours 97, 98

See Echo Lakes tour
(no. 95) for details on
reaching Echo Lakes

241

98 Echo Summit to Fallen Leaf Lake

MAP 38A-38B
PAGE 240-241

Difficulty	5
Length	16 miles one-way
Elevation	7350/+1400,–2050
Navigation	Road, map and compass
Time	Very long day
Season	January through March
USGS topo	7.5′ series, Echo Lake, Pyramid Peak, Rockbound Valley, Emerald Bay
Start	Echo Lake SnoPark. From 1.2 miles west of the Echo Summit Maintenance Station on Highway 50, drive 0.6 mile east towards Berkeley Camp to the SnoPark.
End	From the intersection of Highways 50 and 89 in South Lake Tahoe, drive southwest on Lake Tahoe Blvd. for 2.7 miles and turn right onto Tahoe Mountain Road. Drive 1.1 miles and turn right onto Glenmore Way and then immediately left onto Dundee Circle. In 0.1 mile turn left onto Tahoe Mountain Road once again and park. Do not drive down the narrow plowed portion of Tahoe Mountain Road which is just ahead.

Pyramid Peak and the Crystal Range are among the impressive sights along this extremely long and remote tour. Although snow conditions permit skiing this tour throughout the winter, short days make it difficult to complete in one during mid-winter. Either take two days or wait until the days are longer.

Mileage Log

0.0 – 6.0 +1100,–350 **(1)** Follow the Desolation Valley tour (no. 97) for 6.0 miles until you reach **Lake Aloha (5)**.

6.0 – 7.5 +0 **(5)** Ski northwest along Lake Aloha for 1.5 miles until you reach its **north shore (6)** where Jacks Peak rises abruptly. Exercise caution in the vicinity of Jacks Peak and on both sides of the ridge of which Cracked Crag is dominant; these slopes are subject to avalanche.

7.5 – 7.9 –200 **(6)** Descend east through an obvious notch and just below the steep rise for 0.4 mile until you reach **Heather Lake (7)**.

7.9 – 8.8 –400 **(7)** Cross Heather Lake and then follow its outlet for 0.9 mile until you reach the location where the **creek turns north (8)**.

8.8 – 9.7 –250 **(8)** Continue southeast, paralleling Cracked Crag and the ridge for 0.9 mile until you reach a location **south of Grass Lake (9)** (there is no landmark).

9.7 – 10.6   –450 **(9)** Descend northeast for 0.9 mile until you reach the cabin at **Glen Alpine Spring (10)**. Expect the going to be difficult due to brush and boulders if the snow depth is low.

> *At Glen Alpine Spring you must*
> *locate the road that heads east.*

10.6 – 12.5 –400 **(10)** Descend east on the road for 1.9 miles until you reach the south end **Fallen Leaf Lake (11)**.

12.5 – 15.0 +100 **(11)** Ski north along the east side of Fallen Leaf Lake for 2.5 miles until you reach the junction with **Tahoe Mountain Road (12)**.

15.0 – 15.5 +200 **(12)** Turn east (right) onto Tahoe Mountain Road and climb 0.5 mile until you reach the **ending point (13)** at Dundee Circle.

Desolation Valley   by Gary Clark

99 Lake Audrian

Difficulty	3 from Echo Summit or 2 from Little Norway
Length	3 miles round trip from Echo Summit or 1 mile round trip from Little Norway
Elevation	7400/+250,–250 from Echo Summit or 7200/+50,–50 from Little Norway
Navigation	Road, marked trail and map
Time	Few hours
Season	December through April
USGS topo	7.5′ series, Echo Lake
Start	Echo Summit SnoPark located on the south side of Highway 50, 0.2 mile west of the Echo Summit Maintenance Station. An alternate starting point is Little Norway on Highway 50, 1.0 mile west of the Echo Summit Maintenance Station and 0.2 mile east of the road to Berkeley Camp. The actual starting point is on the south side of the highway, 50 yards east of Little Norway. Be aware that the only building at Little Norway has burned and may be removed.

Years ago, Echo Nordic at Little Norway marked this route on which a few skiers would travel each weekend. Now that the center has closed shop (the building at Little Norway has since burned too), the tour to the lake has almost been forgotten. So ski to the lake and you can be assured of solitude.

Mileage Log

Starting from the Echo Summit SnoPark

0.0 – 0.2   +0 **(1)** Ski north and parallel to the SnoPark entrance road for 0.2 mile until you reach **Highway 50 (2)**. Look for blue diamond markers.

0.2 – 1.0   –200 **(2)** Ski north and gradually turn northwest, paralleling the highway, for 0.8 mile until you reach a **road (3)**. If you lose the markers, just continue by paralleling the highway.

Starting from Little Norway

0.0 – 0.1   +0 **(4)** Locate the road and gate at the Little Norway starting point and ski west on the road for 0.1 mile until you reach the junction with the **route from the Echo Summit SnoPark (3)**. In the event that you pass that intersection, continue to ski on the road for another 0.3 mile until you reach the creek **(5)** that drains Lake Audrian.

*Continuing on the combined routes
with mileages from the SnoPark*

1.0 – 1.3   –50 **(3)** Ski west on the road, away from the highway, for 0.3 mile until you reach the **creek (5)** that drains Lake Audrian. This road is the Sno-Cat route used by the maintenance workers tending the microwave towers on Huckleberry Ridge and is marked with large yellow diamonds.

1.3 – 1.5   +0 **(5)** Turn southeast (left), leave the road, and follow the creek and blue diamonds for 0.2 mile until you reach **Lake Audrian (6)**.

Sharing a snack with a jay   by Herb Steierman

100 Huckleberry Ridge

Difficulty	4
Length	7 miles round trip from Echo Summit or 6 miles round trip from Little Norway
Elevation	7400/+1850,−1850 from Echo Summit or 7200/+1650,−1650 from Little Norway
Navigation	Road, marked trail and map
Time	Full day
Season	December through April
USGS topo	7.5′ series, Echo Lake
Start	Echo Summit SnoPark located on the south side of Highway 50, 0.2 mile west of the Echo Summit Maintenance Station. An alternate starting point is Little Norway on Highway 50, 1.0 mile west of the Echo Summit Maintenance Station and 0.2 mile east of the road to Berkeley Camp. The actual starting point is on the south side of the highway, 50 yards east of Little Norway. Be aware that the only building at Little Norway has burned and may be removed.

Make the tour to Huckleberry Ridge once, and the views and downhill return will bring you back again and again. The climb is steep but tempered by the fact that you have a road to guide you. From either of the microwave towers the views are superb: the Upper Truckee River drainage, Lake Tahoe, Desolation Wilderness and the Crystal Range.

The downhill return is steep and you will find the road narrow, but there are a couple of things that can make the return very enjoyable. The entire ascent, on the steep road, is up a north-facing slope that receives no sun during the mid-winter months. This results in powder that lingers, and mellows the downhill. A treat, for those that can carve turns through steep, forested terrain, is the descent down the nose of the ridge that is also described here.

Mileage Log

Starting from the Echo Summit SnoPark

0.0 – 0.2 +0 (1) Ski north and parallel to the SnoPark entrance road for 0.2 mile until you reach **Highway 50 (2)**. Look for blue diamond markers.

0.2 – 1.0 −200 (2) Ski north and gradually turn northwest, paralleling the highway, for 0.8 mile until you reach a **road (3)**. If you lose the markers, just continue by paralleling the highway.

246

100

Starting from Little Norway

0.0 – 0.1 +0 **(4)** Locate the road and gate at the Little Norway starting point and ski west on the road for 0.1 mile until you reach the junction with the **route from the Echo Summit SnoPark (3)**. In the event that you pass that intersection, continue to ski on the road for another 0.3 mile until you reach the creek (5) that drains Lake Audrian.

Continuing on the combined routes
with mileages from the SnoPark

1.0 – 1.3 –50 **(3)** Ski west on the road, away from the highway, for 0.3 mile until you reach the **creek (5)** that drains Lake Audrian. This road is the Sno-Cat route used by the maintenance workers tending the microwave towers on Huckleberry Ridge and is marked with large yellow diamonds.

1.3 – 1.6 +50 **(5)** Ski west on the road for 0.3 mile until you reach a **sharp left turn (7)**. Beyond here the road and the route climb at a steep angle.

1.6 – 3.2 +1200 **(7)** Climb on the steep road for 1.6 miles until you reach a markedly more **level area on the ridge (8)**.

3.2 – 3.4 +200 **(8)** Ski south, following the markers, for 0.2 mile until you reach the **first microwave tower (9)**.

3.4 – 3.7 +150 **(9)** Ski south and then southwest on the ridge for a total of 0.3 mile until you reach the **second, larger, microwave tower (10)**.

Alternate return route

You can retrace your tracks to the starting point or descend down the nose of Huckleberry Ridge. To do the latter, first return to the level area on the ridge (8). Then descend north on the nose of the ridge for 0.7 mile until you reach the road you previously skied. Then retrace your tracks back to the starting point (1).

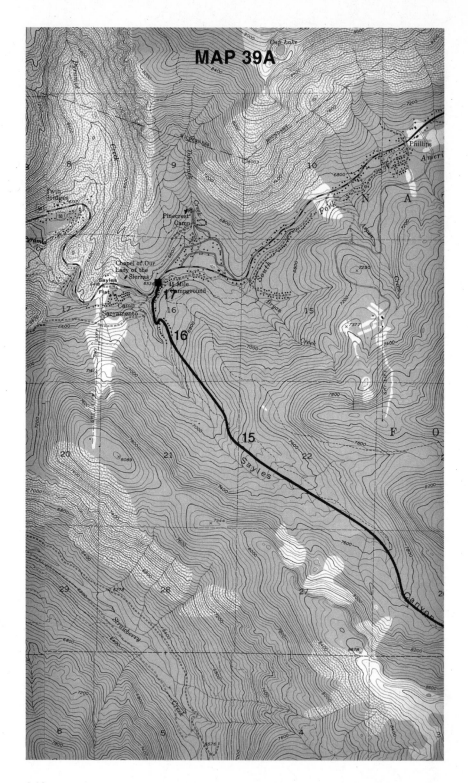

MAP 39A

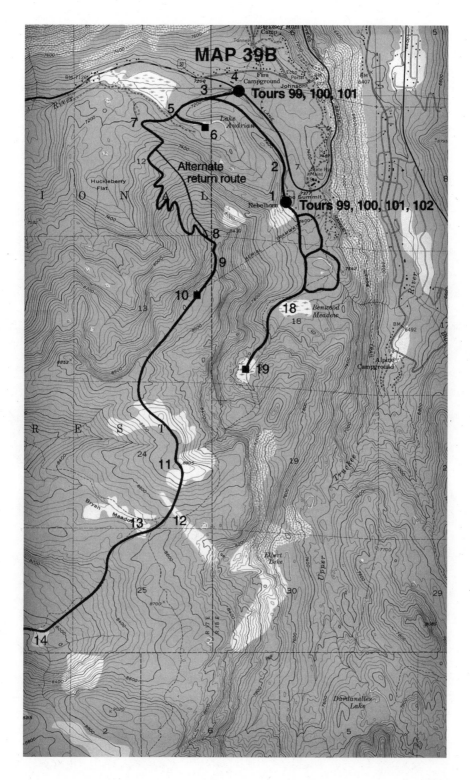

MAP 39B

Tours 99, 100, 101

Tours 99, 100, 101, 102

Alternate
return route

Difficulty	4
Length	11 miles one-way from Echo Summit or 10 miles one-way from Little Norway
Elevation	7400/+2150,–3000 from Echo Summit or 7200/+2150,–2800 from Little Norway
Navigation	Road, marked trail, map and compass
Time	Full day
Season	Late December through mid-April
USGS topo	7.5′ series, Echo Lake
Start	Echo Summit SnoPark located on the south side of Highway 50, 0.2 mile west of the Echo Summit Maintenance Station. An alternate starting point is Little Norway on Highway 50, 1.0 mile west of the Echo Summit Maintenance Station and 0.2 mile east of the road to Berkeley Camp. The actual starting point is on the south side of the highway, 50 yards east of Little Norway. Be aware that the only building at Little Norway has burned and may be removed.
End	Sayles Canyon Tract, 0.4 mile east of Camp Sacramento.

The following synopsis will surely entice advanced skiers to this tour: After a short descent from Echo Summit (none if you begin at Little Norway) you climb 1200 feet to a ridge that overlooks the Upper Truckee River and views of Lake Tahoe. Beyond it is rolling terrain on broad ridges to the highest point of the tour. Ahead is a five-mile, 2400-foot descent. You are guaranteed of solitude, fine views, and a route-finding challenge if you choose this tour.

Mileage Log

0.0 – 3.7   +1600,–250 (**1**) Follow the Huckleberry Ridge tour (no. 100) for 3.7 miles until you reach the **second, larger, microwave tower (10)** at the end of the aerial tramway. Congratulate yourself for having completed the most significant climbing, relax, and enjoy the views.

3.7 – 5.2   +550,–400 (**10**) Follow the ridge southwest and then southeast for a total of 1.5 miles until you reach the **summit of Peak 8905 (11)**.

5.2 – 5.6   –350 (**11**) Descend south, at first through an open area and then through very dense trees for a total of 0.4 mile until you reach a **broad saddle (12)**.

5.6 – 5.8 –50 **(12)** Ski southwest for 0.2 mile until you reach the edge of **Bryan Meadow (13)**.

5.8 – 6.8 –600 **(13)** Descend through the trees to the southwest for 1.0 mile until you reach a **clearing (14)** in the drainage. Be aware that you pass through a couple of small clearings as you descend.

6.8 – 9.1 –700 **(14)** Descend gradually northwest through Sayles Canyon for 2.3 miles until you reach the location where the **drainage becomes noticeable more steep (15)**. Expect a pleasant down-hill run, weaving through the trees as you make quick slalom turns.

9.1 – 10.0 –500 **(15)** Descend the steep canyon for 0.9 mile until you reach a **road (16)**. Although you can ski on either side of the creek as you descend, at the bottom you must be on the east (right) side.

10.0 – 10.6 –150 **(16)** Ski north on the road through a development for 0.6 mile until you reach **Highway 50 (17)**.

Lake Tahoe from microwave tower on Huckleberry Ridge

102 Benwood Meadow

Difficulty	1 – 2
Length	Up to 3 miles round trip
Elevation	7400/Up to +350,–350
Navigation	Map
Time	Few hours
Season	December through April
USGS topo	7.5′ series, Echo Lake
Start	Echo Summit SnoPark located on the south side of Highway 50, 0.2 mile west of the Echo Summit Maintenance Station.

This short, easy tour to a secluded meadow in the Echo Summit area is perfect for beginners. Intermediate skiers can extend the tour a short distance to a higher meadow.

In 1994, volunteers marked two small loops that form a figure-8 near the start of the Benwood Meadow tour. Although not described in detail, they are shown on the map. Regardless of whether you ski these loops, venture east to the rim overlooking the Upper Truckee River drainage to get a glimpse of Lake Tahoe.

Mileage Log

0.0 – 0.8 +50 **(1)** Ski south, climbing gradually at first and then on level terrain, for 0.8 mile until you reach **Benwood Meadow (18)**.

0.8 – 1.3 +300 **(18)** Ski southwest around the west side of Benwood Meadow and then up a drainage for a total of 0.5 mile until you reach a **higher meadow (19)**.

Becker Peak

Nordic Ski Centers

The Nordic centers listed here provide ski touring services and facilities, and are a good source for current snow, weather and avalanche conditions.

CLAIR TAPPAAN LODGE
Location   South of Interstate 80 on Donner Pass Road at Norden.
Phone   916-426-3632
Elevation   7000'

DIAMOND PEAK CROSS COUNTRY
Location   Mt. Rose Highway, 5 miles north of Incline Village.
Phone   702-831-3211 and 702-832-1177
Elevation   8100'

EAGLE MOUNTAIN NORDIC
Location   South of Interstate 80 at the Yuba Gap exit and 20 miles west of Donner Pass.
Phone   916-389-2254 and 800-391-2254
Elevation   5750'

NORTHSTAR-AT-TAHOE
Location   Off Highway 267, halfway between Truckee and Lake Tahoe, at Northstar-At-Tahoe ski resort.
Phone   916-562-1330 and 916-562-2475
Elevation   6400'

ROYAL GORGE CROSS COUNTRY SKI RESORT
Location   South of Interstate 80 on Donner Pass Road at Soda Springs.
Phone   916-426-3871
Elevation   7000'

SPOONER LAKE CROSS COUNTRY
Location   Spooner Lake picnic area, 1 mile north of the junction of Highways 28 and 50, and 10 miles south of Incline Village.
Phone   702-887-8844 and 749-5349
Elevation   7000'

SQUAW CREEK CROSS COUNTRY
Location   The Resort at Squaw Valley on Squaw Creek Road in Squaw Valley.
Phone   916-583-6300
Elevation   6200'

TAHOE DONNER CROSS COUNTRY

Location   Two miles west of downtown Truckee and four miles north on Northwoods Blvd.

Phone   916-587-9494 and 916-587-9484

Elevation   6600'

TAHOE NORDIC SKI CENTER

Location   Two miles east of Tahoe City on Highway 28 and four blocks behind the Dollar Hill Shell gas station.

Phone   916-583-0484 and 583-9858

Elevation   6600'

A great day with friends   by Lee Griffith

Updates

Here is your opportunity to keep your *Ski Tours in the Sierra Nevada* guidebooks up-to-date.

Send a self-addressed, stamped, number 10 envelope to Bittersweet Publishing Company. Indicate the volume(s) for which you want to receive updates. You will be mailed updates when they become available.

Bittersweet Publishing Company
P.O. Box 1211
Livermore, California 94551